The Art of Commercial Lending

Edgar M. Morsman Jr.

rma
THE RISK MANAGEMENT ASSOCIATION
Serving the Financial Services Industry

Philadelphia, PA

About RMA

RMA is the association of lending and credit risk professionals. Founded in 1914, RMA has grown more than 3,000 commercial banks and thrift institutions, which account for nearly 80% of the C&I lending done by U.S. commercial banks.These institutions are represented in the association by more than 18,000 commercial loan and credit officers and related personnel in all 50 states, Puerto Rico, Canada, and several offshore cities.

RMA was originally named after Robert Morris, the American patriot who signed the Declaration of Independence, was largely responsible for the financing of our Revolutionary War, and helped establish our banking system.

The association's original purpose back in 1914 was to facilitate the flow and interchange of credit information. Today, this purpose has been expanded to include working continuously to improve the principles and practices of commercial lending, loan management, credit administration, and related areas in its member institutions and others in the financial services industry.

RMA seeks to fulfill its purpose by providing commercial bankers with programs, products, and services they need to increase their proficiency in lending, credit, and related areas RMA's reason for being, then, is to provide these bankers with the tools they need to make better loans, keep abreast of the continual changes that affect the lending function, and, at the bottom line, help them increase the profit ability of their institutions.

Library of Congress Cataloging-in-Publication Data

Morsman, Edgar Martin
The Art of Commercial Lending / Edgar M. Morsman, Jr.
p. cm.
Includes bibliographical references (p.).
ISBN 1-57070-017-6 (paperback)
1. Commercial loans. 2. Bank management. 3. Bank employees--Training of. I. Title.
HG1641.M78 1997
332.1'2'068—dc21 97-24752

While RMA believes the material contained in this publication is accurate, the conclusions and opinions expressed are those of the author. Moreover, no opinion expressed on a legal matter should be relied on without the advice of counsel familiar with both the facts in a particular case and the applicable law.

Additional copies of this publication are available from the Customer Relations,RMA, One Liberty Place, Suite 2300, Philadelphia, PA 19103-7398 800-677-7621.

Printed on recycled paper.

Contents

Foreword

RMA is pleased to publish Ed Morsman's latest work for new lending personnel: account managers, relationship managers, and first-line supervisors of these key figures in the lending and credit intermediation process. Calling on his 33 years' experience in the banking industry as a bank CEO, senior credit executive, and lender, Morsman hits all the key areas a lender must manage to be effective and successful in today's financial services industry environment.

Morsman's premise is simple: Being successful as a lender requires mastery of many diverse skills, including self-management, channeling institutional resources, and handling the intricate internal and external relationships ranging from prospecting new customers to closing a deal. Marketing savvy, proper framing and structuring of borrower's requests, successful presentation of these requests for institutional approval and underwriting, managing the market, and managing internal interrelationships for optimal results all add up to an invaluable and timeless reference piece for readers new to commercial lending.

This latest work completes a trilogy of writings by Morsman. His first book, *Effective Loan Management*, deals with the responsibilities of mid-level managers in the lending and credit process; his second book, *Commercial Loan Portfolio Management*, describes the means by which top management sets the course for an institution to successfully realize its desired results via the credit intermediation process. *The Art of Commercial Lending*, appropriately completes the trilogy by addressing individual tasks and contributions necessary to achieve both personal and institutional success.

ACKNOWLEDGMENTS

RMA wishes to thank Edgar M. Morsman Jr., past president of RMA for his lifetime contributions to the literature of the industry. Throughout his career, Morsman has been a regular supplier of articles, speeches, and publications of great interest and importance to those associated with commercial lending. This book, *The Art of Commercial Lending*, will help future generations of bankers achieve excellence needed in today's market. Thank you, Ed, for your lifelong willingness to share your savvy with others.

Finally, RMA is indebted to the following bankers who served on the review committee for the manuscript: Sloan Gibson, AmSouth Bank of Alabama; Sonny Lyles, Bank United; Doug Nelson, Bank One, Texas, N.A.; and Lee O'Neill, Busey Bank. Every reader in the industry knows the heavy demands facing banking executives today. Therefore, those who willingly perform a voluntary type of service such as serving on a reviewing committee deserve our special thanks and appreciation. To these four executives, RMA wishes to express, on behalf of the author and the association, its gratitude for a job well done.

Credit & Risk Management
RMA
Philadelphia, Pennsylvania

Preface

Despite the time and effort spent on highly analytical issues such as statement spreading and the resultant ratio and trend analysis, commercial lending remains an art, not a science. In fact, commercial lending has become one of the last areas of financing that have not succumbed to credit-scoring and other forms of data mining.

I do not mean to say that more objective and analytical techniques cannot be introduced into the art of lending to businesses. Indeed, certain techniques are discussed in later chapters. Nevertheless, the commercial lender is daily faced with the challenge of meshing the specific needs of customers with bank policies that are rarely, if ever, highly specific.

Thus, as a commercial banker, you must create tailor-made solutions that are competitive while meeting the needs of the customer and the financial institution. There are no one-size-fits-all solutions. Compounding the challenge, you must operate in an environment with a certain amount of ambiguity while producing results that must be correct 99.5% of the time, since commercial lending is rarely profitable if the net loan loss ratio exceeds 0.5% over a business cycle.

The job description of a commercial banker engaged in relationship management is highly complex. Few positions in any industry combine responsibilities for sales, credit, pricing, collection, and customer service into one job. The potential for conflict in these responsibilities is obvious.

Commercial bankers are, therefore, navigating between customer desires and bank policies in a sea of ambiguity where unique and creative solutions must be crafted, negotiated, and sold. Your job is similar to an artisan's, and like an artisan, you create and sign the final result.

THE IDEAL ENVIRONMENT

An artisan must be trained in basic fundamentals and disciplines and then be assigned to an apprenticeship where creativity can be developed through coaching and counseling in a nurturing environment. In a similar manner, commercial bankers gain analytical skills in basic training programs. However, the real development of the lending art comes from guided hands-on experience in a caring line unit.

This book is not about basic analytical skills. Rather, it focuses on the relatively inexperienced commercial banker and how he or she and the appropriate manager can maximize career development and results with a customer and market base in a confusing internal and external environment.

After intense basic training in such areas as credit analysis, product knowledge, and organizational objectives, you should hope to be placed in a line unit with the following characteristics:

- Admission is highly selective, and team members view themselves as members of an elite unit.
- The mission of the unit is clear and standards are high; everyone understands what is expected of all team members.
- Team members are given challenging opportunities early in their careers with constant feedback on performance, so skills are under constant development.
- Team members are encouraged to take reasonable risks as well as seek creative solutions and innovations.
- Teamwork is emphasized, and there is total honesty in performance evaluation.
- Continuous training, development, coaching, and counseling are a way of life.
- The team focuses on excellence and quality and believes that customer satisfaction is as important as profitability.

THE ROLE OF LEADERSHIP

Such a unit is created by a leader, not a manager. While a manager makes the most of the status quo, a leader takes people where they have never been before. In the highly regulated environment of banking in past decades, good managers could, indeed, make a real difference in a static environment. They were successful through their administration of systems, processes, and controls.

Although solid administration is still critical, a rapidly changing environment requires that people and organizations evolve to survive. People resist change because they have a vested interest in the status quo. The leader must articulate a new vision and strategy for the organization and enroll team members in the new order of things. The leader shows team members how to let go of the old and stretch for the new.

The leader is a facilitator, a mentor, one who provides strategy and direction while coaching, counseling, and providing feedback. The leader recognizes and encourages, resolves conflicts, and gives authority and resources.

LESS THAN IDEAL ENVIRONMENTS

The benefits of starting a commercial banking career in a well-led unit focusing on excellence are obvious. However, the demands on managers are so great that most fall somewhat short of perfection while still achieving adequate results. Once a manager worried primarily about the budget and credit quality. Today a manager also must be concerned with sales management, technology changes, competitive pressure on risks and rewards, quality, customer satisfaction, productivity, and human resource development. It is a rare person, indeed, who can master all requirements. In addition, a number of practices conspire against them:

- In most people's eyes, the rewards system, or how people are compensated, promoted, and recognized, represents the real value system of an organization. If management professes an empowered environment that strives for excellence but rewards people only for hitting their numbers and producing clean audits, then coaching, counseling, and the development of people will be fairly low on a manager's list of activities. Management's real priorities are transparent, and the reward system reflects them.

- Banking does not have an abundance of exceptional leaders or empowered organizations to follow, so there are few role models. Until the 1980s, banking was a heavily regulated, stagnate environment in which managers made the most of the status quo. At his retirement party in the late 1970s, one bank president remarked that the greatest change he had encountered in his banking career was air conditioning. Many people who grew up managing in a stable environment are ill equipped to cope with rapid change. It is a credit to the industry that banking has developed a number of truly enlightened leaders who are directing empowered organizations.

- Business tends to promote the best individual performers to management positions even when they demonstrate little aptitude or even desire for the position. The skills necessary to succeed in management are very different from the skills necessary to succeed in commercial lending. Why would anyone accept a job he or she did not want? In banking, management is generally the only route to recognition and rewards. Unlike insurance or the brokerage business, banking has struggled to figure out how to reward the individual producer, so the system forces people into management. The outcome is frequently the loss of a good producer and the creation of a poor manager who often falls back on his or her best skill, commercial lending, and ignores subordinates.

- Many newly promoted managers fail, despite every good intention, because they have received no training or have no role models to emulate. Management requires the same skill development as that of a producer or specialist. Most managers are player/coaches and maintaining the appropriate balance can be extremely challenging.
- Although a significant part of management's job is intangible—creating a vision, building a culture, exercising judgment—the belief persists that if it cannot be measured, do not bother with it. Consequently, many irrelevant and trivial issues are measured, while intangible, yet crucial, activities such as training, coaching, counseling, and developing people are ignored. This management malpractice can have a devastating long-term effect on employees and ensure that significant openings are filled from the outside.

PURPOSE OF THIS BOOK

This book assumes that it is a statistically good bet that most novice commercial bankers will land in a less than perfect environment, and, therefore, it offers suggestions on creating a positive development experience. The fundamental premise is that you can learn much from your manager and team, but you also are responsible for your development and self-management..

In a cooperative environment, the commercial banker has a responsibility beyond self and that is to the team and its leader. Consequently, this book also focuses on contributing to a team effort and helping the manager do a better job in leading people. Your challenge is compounded by dealing in a highly competitive external market while negotiating through the occasional internal obstacles erected by peers, managers, credit committees, and the ubiquitous policies, procedures, regulations, and audit controls.

While the book is aimed at the novice commercial banker, managers should benefit by seeing themselves through the eyes of their subordinates. Senior management should be able to use this book to derive better expectations of their managers, and staff credit and loan review personnel should gain insights into the complexities of the commercial banking job.

SUMMARY OF THE CHAPTERS

Chapter 1 illustrates some of the self-management principles that the novice commercial banker should master as these techniques will help shape an entire career.

Chapter 2 examines issues related to making the most out of meeting the customer and developing this base of business.

Chapter 3 outlines techniques for establishing marketing goals and maximizing prospecting and sales efforts.

Chapter 4 illustrates methods of examining loan requests and structuring them so they meet both customer needs and bank policy.

Chapter 5 discusses managing the internal loan approval process from writing a succinct approval document to negotiating through the credit committee.

Chapter 6 focuses on documenting and closing the transaction from designing appropriate covenants to orchestrating a successful closing while collaborating with lawyers.

Chapter 7 proposes methods of allocating precious time in the external environment between existing customers and prospects based on actual and potential profitability.

Chapter 8 examines managing the internal environment in such areas as performance evaluation, career development, and mentoring.

A questionnaire in the appendix sets forth a nonthreatening tool with which the banker and the manager can examine a commercial banking function and set priorities and responsibilities for change.

ACKNOWLEDGMENTS

A 33-year career in financial services has given me the opportunity to practice an art that if done appropriately, enhances wealth, creates employment, and expands opportunity, all within a framework of integrity and concern for others. I am indebted to Norwest Corporation and its management, staff, and customers for its encouragement of excellence, innovation, and prudent risk-taking. I would also like to commend RMA, which, in its capacity as the conscience of the industry, has provided invaluable career development opportunities as well as life-long friendships.

Edgar M. Morsman Jr.
Minneapolis, Minnesota

Chapter 1

Getting Started

Congratulations! You have just been made a commercial banker and have entered one of the most exciting and fascinating arenas in financial services. What makes commercial banking unique is also one of its challenges—its ambiguity. When reviewing an opportunity, you must learn to deal with policies that may be unwritten and shaped by the culture and personalities of management and team members. The ability to tolerate and thrive in a certain amount of ambiguity is a prerequisite of the job.

To be effective, you also must establish some life-long work habits or disciplines early in your career. As with sports or music, certain disciplines must be practiced until they become instinctive. This chapter focuses on three work habits—managing time well, maintaining good working relationships, and ensuring self-education. Others will be introduced later in the book.

Working on these disciplines from the start is critical to your ultimate success. Good habits and disciplines, like golf and tennis strokes, may seem unnatural and uncomfortable at first. Frankly, mastering good work habits is neither interesting nor fun. However, they must be acquired early in your career; your chances of developing them later are not very good.

MANAGING TIME

The first observation you will make in your new position is that the demands on your available time take on a menacing new form. Instead of prepackaged modules of case studies you may have encountered as a student or trainee, you must now develop all the information yourself, put it into logical form, and then draw conclusions that must be sold to others. In addition, instead of an orderly series of tasks with a beginning, end, and debriefing, you are bombarded by a constant and overwhelming stream of random demands.

Rarely can you work on one task until completion and then start another one. Unfortunately, your prioritizing skills may not be well developed yet and not much guidance is available. Also, you have not had time to develop resources and networks for problem solving, so you cannot work particularly efficiently.

Real time feedback is elusive, so you may not always know if you are establishing the right priorities or doing the job according to expectations. In sum, you are operating in a fog with occasional glimmers of sunlight that are frequently obscured by shifts in the vapor.

Don't despair. This atmosphere is perfectly normal at first. You should be able to put some order into this chaos within six months, but it will require real self-discipline, including the effective management of time. Time is a precious and nonrenewable resource. You must make it serve you rather than be a slave to it.

STRUCTURING THE DAY

Most commercial bankers find it efficient to establish some general structure to the day based on their energy levels and the rhythm of their organizations. Of course, this structure is not inviolate. Interruptions and crises may make the general structure feel like the exception rather than the rule at times. Accept these unexpected events with equanimity. In fact, there are at least three occasions when you should drop everything you are doing and attend to the challenge at hand:

- A sales opportunity.
- A customer service problem.
- A credit problem.

Nevertheless, some basic structure to the day is a habit that will greatly enhance efficiency. For example, if your energy level is highest in the morning, tackle work that requires creativity such as credit or sales proposals.

Lunch is an ideal time for customer and prospect development or networking with others in the organization. Make a point of developing this habit early rather than falling into a pattern of lunching with the same comfortable crowd every day.

Afternoons might be devoted to lower energy undertakings such as administrative issues and calling for customer and prospect appointments. Late afternoons and some time in the evening might be a good time for professional reading or other self-training opportunities.

Putting some basic structure into the day eventually becomes instinctive and painlessly increases efficiency. In deciding your own structure, observe what co-workers are doing and adapt what makes sense. Also, talk to peers you admire about how they structure the day. Most will be delighted to give you their thoughts.

EVALUATING THE USE OF TIME

Most individuals think of the calendar as a means of keeping track of commitments and ensuring that they are fulfilled. This approach tells you what you are doing, not what you should be doing. An equally important, but rarely used, purpose of the calendar is to examine and evaluate the past to determine how effectively time has been managed. This exercise is essential to improving your time management habits in the future.

To begin, consider the basic components of the income statement—net interest income, noninterest income, loan loss provision, noninterest income, and noninterest expense. These components suggest three basic work functions: sales, credit, and administration.

Sales efforts are reflected in net interest income and noninterest income. Net interest income is a function of volume and pricing or the interest spread and configuration of the maturities of loan assets and funding sources. Noninterest income comes from nonloan-related fees such as cash management, trust, and international activities. Net interest income and noninterest income drive the income statement, so sales efforts should receive the most significant portion of your time and effort.

Credit efforts are reflected in the provision for loan loss, which in most commercial lending functions should fall within a range of 0.25% to 0.75%. This small tolerance for error means, on average, you can only be wrong about 0.5% of the time—a very small target. Increasing risk only makes sense if you can increase reward, which is difficult in an industry with overcapacity. Until the number of banks reaches equilibrium with available business, commercial loan portfolios must be extremely clean to be profitable.

Credit results are more a reflection of the credit culture and management intentions than the amount of paper generated by the credit process. The time spent on the credit process must be judged for the value it adds rather than the time it consumes.

Administrative efforts are reflected in noninterest expenses, which are primarily salary and benefits but also include such expenses as office, communications, travel, data processing, entertainment, and allocations from other areas of the bank including management. When salary and benefit expenses are involved in sales activities or credit activities that add value, they are productive and enhance earnings. Time devoted to other activities generally detracts from earnings.

Although no reliable industry data exist, an educated estimate of time allocated in most commercial banking activities would put approximately one-third in sales, one-third in credit, and one-third in administration. Reliable data are scarce because of the difficulty of agreeing in what function activities should fall. For example, many banks find that only half of their lenders' sales time is actually spent face to face with customers. The rest is spent in writing reports, going to sales meetings, doing research, and so forth. Should these activities be allocated to sales or administration? The point is that only about one-sixth of total time is actually spent with customers or prospects.

Unfortunately, there is no main culprit in administrative efforts that can be hacked out to increase efficiency. The one-third of time devoted to administration is made up of tiny increments and tasks that do not seem much in themselves but add up to a staggering distraction from profitability.

Although many banks are reevaluating their commercial lending functions with the view of making them more efficient, there is little you can or should do about it until you gain experience and establish credibility. At such time, it will be your obligation to suggest means of making the unit more efficient. Individuals at the line level are in the best position to recommend changes.

Although there is little you can immediately do to improve systems, there is a great deal you can do about understanding how you use your time and how you should be using it. At the end of each week, probably before you go home Friday evening, evaluate how you managed time during the week. At a minimum, examine your usage of time and the degree of procrastination. Then examine your plans for the next week and make necessary adjustments. This exercise takes only a few minutes.

Using your calendar for the past week, divide the time you spent into sales, credit, and administrative segments and calculate a percentage for each. Obviously, you will make some arbitrary decisions, which is not a problem as long as you remain consistent. Write the percentages on your calendar. What were they and what would you like them to be? What drives the allocation? What factors can you control? What is the trend?

Then examine your to-do list. You need to determine if it is challenging enough to fulfill your objectives and if you are accomplishing your tasks in a timely fashion. Does your calendar for the next week reflect what you are striving to accomplish and how you should be spending your time?

Only you can manage your time, and it is critical that you establish time management disciplines early, so they become instinctive. It is extremely difficult to recognize and change bad habits once they are ingrained.

Two final thoughts on time management. First, you should gradually establish a reasonable balance between your professional and personal life. This balance should be created with the agreement and support of those close to you. Commercial banking, or any other exciting position, can become a seductive narcotic. Unfortunately, careers end or change direction through circumstances beyond one's control. A balanced life style can make finding new directions much less intimidating.

Second, and in apparent contradiction, there are times when you must ignore your balance and devote a disproportionate amount of time to the office, especially when you take on a new position or challenge regardless of where your are in your career path. In any new job, you must learn new skills and overcome initial inefficiency. You must make those close to you understand that learning the ropes takes about six months and then you anticipate returning to the agreed-on balance.

WORKING RELATIONSHIPS

Your entry into a unit changes the status quo. You will affect team performance, workloads, and perceptions both inside and outside the organization. Change makes people uncomfortable at first, so you must be sensitive to developing positive relationships with support personnel, peers, and your manager.

ADMINISTRATIVE SUPPORT

One serious mistake some individuals make, either intentionally or unintentionally, is to fail to treat all members of the organization with equal thoughtfulness and respect. In a good organization, all positions, from janitor to CEO, have an essential purpose and should be filled with qualified personnel.

As an account manager orchestrating the resources of the organization on behalf of customers, you will eventually need the assistance of many individuals, including those you do not control in a hierarchical sense. Treat everyone as if you will need their help at some point. You probably will.

Administrative assistants are frequently under pressure because they serve the needs of several people with conflicting needs and priorities. Stress is caused by the inability to control events. When you join a unit, take the time to discuss work routines with assistants and how to recognize and resolve conflicts. Talk to them periodically about what is going right and wrong and how improvements can be made.

One of your challenges is ensuring that you are engaged in a significant portion of high value-added activities. As you evaluate your use of time, consider whether some of the work you are doing could be more appropriately handled by support staff. In particular, examine your usage of the personal computer.

The personal computer is a wonderful vehicle for such tasks as scheduling, messaging, data retrieval, standardized correspondence, and so forth. However, when managers see the same individuals constantly tapping away at the computer, they begin to question why they are not out with customers or prospects. Make sure the computer is a tool to increase the value of your time. If it is not, ask if someone else is more appropriate for the work you are doing.

PEERS

Your first six months on the job are generally bewildering and occasionally frustrating. You must learn new skills, processes, resources, and the unwritten rules of the game. Although a good manager can help guide you through this thicket, he or she is rarely available to respond in a timely fashion to all the questions you have.

Consequently, you must develop productive relationships with peers who can assist you. Look for opportunities to reciprocate. Peer relationships also should be cultivated in other areas such as trust, operations, and marketing where you need resources and assistance. Do not overlook lunchtime opportunities to build these relationships.

With strong peer relationships, you do not need to be present at all contacts with your customer base. Problems or opportunities are best handled by those with the requisite skills. A good relationship manager ensures that a customer has multiple contacts within the bank.

YOUR MANAGER

When you are operating in an ambiguous environment, receiving timely feedback from your manager is extremely helpful. Making slight, but frequent, midcourse corrections is much more effective than waiting all year for a performance appraisal and then attempting a major shift in direction.

To receive helpful feedback, you must actively seek it. Assembling a group of managers and new commercial bankers demonstrates the problem. When asked, managers state that they give constant feedback to new bankers on their behaviors. The new bankers look on in wonderment and say they rarely receive feedback, which is one of the reasons why the first six months on the job are so confusing.

What is happening and who is correct? Generally, managers give less feedback than they think. Commercial bankers deal with constant controversy and conflict through credit issues, pricing, budgets, and competitive factors. If managers feel that feedback will produce more controversy and conflict, it is human nature to avoid it.

On the other hand, new commercial bankers do receive more feedback than they realize because many are just not listening. They tend to be so focused on the task at hand that they miss the subtleties in which feedback is often couched.

What should you do? Now is the time to diplomatically and systematically ask for feedback not just from your manager but from your peers as well. For example, returning from a customer or prospect call is an excellent opportunity for a debriefing. Don't ask, "How did I do?" You should not be fishing for compliments, particularly if your colleague has something else in mind. Ask for suggestions on making the call more productive. When the feedback starts flowing, listen carefully and watch your body language. Never become defensive or argumentative; it is a sure way to shut off feedback once and for all. If, after careful thought, you find that the feedback is unhelpful because it does not suit your style, make a mental note to reject it. Don't turn the occasion into conflict.

If you were taking golf or tennis lessons from a pro, you would be paying to receive helpful feedback. Make your manager and peers understand that you are in a learning experience and that as pros, you welcome and respect their feedback. If you don't help them do their jobs, you will be missing an important learning opportunity.

EDUCATION

Banking has traditionally provided fairly intense entry-level training, while more advanced education has been on a sporadic and unsystematic basis. With the rapid changes in the financial services environment, education cannot end with placement in a job. You are primarily responsible for your continuing education, as you are best able to recognize shortcomings and know how much time you are willing to devote to it.

You should begin your continuing education with a sound professional reading program that might include some of or all the following:

- A newspaper covering your local market.
- A business journal covering local or national events.
- A business weekly magazine.

- An industry newspaper.
- A professional publication such as the *Journal of Lending & Credit Risk Management*.

As you progress in your career, you should periodically evaluate your reading program to ensure it meets your current needs. It is important that you establish this discipline immediately even though you are incredibly pressed for time.

Other educational needs will become apparent after you have gained some experience on the job. If your organization does not have a formal continuing education program, suggest some training opportunities to your manager. Most organizations are happy to meet the training needs of their employees. However, the initiative must often come from you.

SUMMARY

The first 6 to 12 months of a commercial banking job is normally a bewildering experience of learning new skills and processes in an ambiguous environment. Learning the ropes can be so challenging and time-consuming that life-long habits and disciplines are frequently ignored. These disciplines include managing time, maintaining good working relationships, and pursuing continuing education.

If these disciplines can be made instinctive, you will operate much more effectively and find the challenges of the job rewarding and enjoyable.

Chapter 2

Meeting the Customer

Now it is time to meet the customer, an event that should never cease to inspire awe, respect, and anticipation on the part of the commercial banker. The customer is the reason for the existence of your organization, and you must never forget it. Great companies are always focused on the customer, yet even great companies, as well as industries, occasionally lose this focus and turn inward. Inevitably, they slip into mediocrity and disappear through acquisition or, in rare cases, are resuscitated by great leaders.

The best commercial bankers always consider working with the customer or prospect challenging and fascinating and that is where they want to spend their time. If you do not feel this way, you are probably in the wrong business. Dealing successfully with customers is, of course, where the money is made, so an excessive internal focus on trivia is an unprofitable diversion.

As a new account officer, your introduction to a customer base will fall somewhere between serving an apprenticeship to being handed a customer list with the comment, "Let me know if you have any questions." In more placid and regulated times, many commercial bankers did start as apprentices to experienced senior bankers and were gradually worked into a customer and prospect base. With acquisitions, reorganizations, and turnover, many new commercial bankers are thrust directly into customer contact. In effect, they are being trained at the expense of their banks' customers.

Managing significant turnover is the bane of all managers and a constant complaint of customers. An institution that puts the same bankers before the same customers for a reasonable period of time will have stronger relationships, greater cross sales, better credit, and higher profits than an institution with high turnover. In relationship banking, it is very difficult to establish good relationships when the partners keep changing.

With high turnover, there is less time for hands-on coaching, counseling, and apprenticing of new bankers. Consequently, you must again rely on developing self-management skills.

PREPARING FOR A CALL

How you prioritize your calls depends, to a great extent, on how you are introduced to your new customers. Ideally, you will be introduced by the previous account officer or your manager, or both.

However, the previous account officer may be moving on to a new challenge in the organization, so his or her time and interest may be limited. Therefore, you must prioritize your calls using three screens:

1. *Profitability*. The importance of account profitability systems is discussed in Chapter 7. However, if your bank is operating without one, you are at a significant disadvantage. You will not have the time to devise a system now, so rough approximations based on interest earned, demand deposit balances, other fees, and such must suffice. Do not overlook profitable nonborrowing customers.

2. *Credit issues*. Discuss the credit quality of the list with the previous account officer and a member of loan review to determine which accounts have credit issues that need addressing. Also, highlight any customers that have a credit request or other change in the relationship in process.

3. *Vendor or partner relationship*. With the help of the previous account officer, designate customers by whether they treat the bank as a vendor to be called when a bid is requested or a partner at the planning table. Obviously, the profit potential of the latter is significantly greater and should rank the customer higher on your call priority list. This approach is discussed further in Chapter 7.

How much time you can spend on your calls dictates their content. For example, is your first call just a quick introduction or a plant tour or planning session? You will probably have little control over the time available for joint calls, so you may need to plan follow-up calls on your own. If you cannot schedule joint calls with the entire customer list, the previous account officer should write introductory letters to customers you have not met stating that you will schedule a meeting shortly.

Once you have scheduled your calls, you should immediately begin to prepare for them. This preparation is time-consuming and arduous, but it pays big dividends. Fortunately, much of this preparation need not be repeated for future calls. The obvious place to start your preparation is the credit file.

CREDIT FILES

The term *credit file* is used in a generic sense. Before the advent of personal computers, virtually all documentation relating to a customer's relationship was contained in a credit file. The file was frequently a miniature landfill containing financial statements, spreadsheets, correspondence, call memos, credit presentations, newspaper clippings, catalogs, and miscellaneous detritus. With the advent of improved technology, this debris may now be scattered among several systems ranging from papers in the credit file to call memos on a relationship accounting system to financial data on a spreading program.

Unless you have spent some time in operations, you are most likely unaware of the cost of retaining this information. The costs are spread through many different areas, including occupancy expense for space and storage equipment, clerical help for filing, technical help for data storage and retrieval, increased storage capacity, and emergency backup systems. These costs tend to return to the commercial banking department through inscrutable budgeted allocations. Consequently, account officers cannot relate their actions to ultimate costs.

As you plow through the credit file data, you will formulate some conclusions about the artisanship and analytical abilities of the author. In fact, reading credit files is one of the key methods of assessing skill levels when conducting due diligence in an acquisition. This knowledge should provide you with sufficient incentive to be careful about your construction of credit files and the management of data. Your manager also monitors your files and draws conclusions about your artisanship as a commercial banker. You will do the same should you become a manager. If the files you are reading are good, learn from them. If they are not, vow to do better.

As you read the credit files, try to understand who the decision makers in the company are and if you will see them on your call. If you do not meet with the decision makers, leave your business card for them during the call and follow up on your next visit.

You also should gain a sense of the call history on the customer and decide whether it makes sense for the priorities you have established. Start thinking about appropriate calling frequency and what other members of the team should be included from senior management to specialists in such areas as cash management, trust, and trade finance.

Of course, you should examine the financial statements of the customer and its borrowing history. Try to formulate a mental image of what the customer's place of business might look like. For example, relate the inventory and sales volume to the fixed assets and equipment available to house it. What kind of production and office space do you think is required? Will existing trends change these relationships?

As a trainee, you probably considered financial statements as abstractions or realities that should be analyzed as if they were entities unto themselves. Unfortunately, many commercial bankers still consider financial statements in that light. However, you are not lending to financial statements. You should now begin to think of financial statements as one way of viewing an underlying economic reality—your customer. Although highly useful as a tool, financial statements only present your customer in historic financial terms. Get in the habit of using financial statements as just one of the tools you must use to understand your customer.

Formulating a mental image of the customer through an examination of the statements is one means of getting into that habit. When you call on the customer and discover that your mental image is off base, reexamine the financials to discover the reason for your misperception.

OTHER RESOURCES

Commercial bankers are often so involved in lending that they do not have a good understanding of how a customer uses and views its bank. An obvious place to develop this insight is with the deposit functions. Examine your deposit reports to obtain a sense of the cash flows of the customer. Is your bank the sole depository or does the company use you only for disbursements? If some other institution has the cash collection business, who is it and why don't you have it?

Find out what other services the customer is using and talk to the providers. You want to understand the profitability of other services, find additional sales potential, and uncover any friction points. Most likely, your customer will not be open to listening to a new sales pitch if there is a controversy raging in another department.

You also should check with your purchasing department to learn if your customer is a vendor of your bank and if not, if it should be considered. Purchasing departments are notorious for causing customer problems. In one bank, the purchasing department was receiving kudos for the cash it was generating by slowing the payables turn. However, the asset-based lending department of the same bank was faced with declaring ineligible the same bank receivables on the customer's books. You also may find that your bank is giving considerable business to a customer that is giving you little in return. The purchasing department's vendor list also is a good source for prospects.

Finally, talk to prior account officers before the call because many subtleties will not be in the credit files. You should ask about negotiating styles, common objections, "hot buttons" such as pricing, friction points, competitive aspects, sales opportunities, and so forth. A member of the loan review department also may have some solid insights into your customer base, and reviewing the list over lunch is usually worthwhile.

THEME OF THE CALL

Every call should have a theme or purpose. As you prepare for a call, think of three to five specific objectives or questions you might want answered. Questions could relate to sales opportunities or credit issues. The objectives should be defined narrowly enough so that they can be reasonably accomplished. For example, you may think of qualifying a customer for a specific cash management product and arranging a call by a specialist. Or you may be concerned with the quality of inventory and want assurances on certain issues.

Most customers have a specific theme, challenge, or opportunity that is reflected in their financial results and management styles. These themes may involve such issues as sales growth outstripping financial and managerial resources, management succession, adapting to changing markets, or estate planning. Identifying these themes is important because the themes affect your strategy with the customer.

As you prepare, try to identify the dominant theme of the customer. You may not have the opportunity to confirm it on your first call, especially if it is a quick introduction, but you should get in the habit of identifying dominant issues early in your career.

PLANNING WITH YOUR MANAGER

The alert manager will want to join you and the previous account officer on as many calls on your new customers as possible. The occasion provides the manager with an opportunity to accomplish many objectives with minimal effort. For example:

- *Customer rapport.* These calls enhance the manager's rapport with the customer base. Because the calls have been prioritized, the manager sees customers that have the most impact on the profit center. These calls also give the customers the opportunity to know the manager better. If there is a problem with the relationship, the manager would rather hear about it directly than have the customer go to a competitor.

- *Relationship status.* The manager can learn firsthand whether there are any concerns over the change in account officers. This meeting is an excellent opportunity to obtain a report card on the relationship and learn of any problems or issues. For example, there may be a festering controversy in another department that could poison the whole relationship.
- *Additional support.* If you are particularly inexperienced, the manager can attempt to elevate you in the eyes of the customer and demonstrate that you have the authority, support, and resources necessary to meet the customer's needs. Although you are primarily responsible for the relationship, your manager's presence at the meeting lets the customer know he or she can always call on the manager in case of need.
- *Coaching opportunity.* These first calls permit the manager to see you in action and provide coaching and counseling opportunities in a constructive and informal manner. The car ride back to the bank is often a good opportunity for suggestions and discussions of the outcome of the call. Frequent, nonthreatening, on-the-spot coaching and counseling is the most productive method of providing feedback and changing behavior.

ESTABLISHING YOUR ROLE

Assuming your manager joins you on at least some of your calls, you need to establish what role you are to play in front of the customer. You may be a ball carrier, a bag carrier, or somewhere in between. The good manager wants you to play an active role in the call so that your authority is established when you are working with the customer on your own. The manager also wants to observe how you operate and then do some informal coaching.

Unfortunately, some managers, even with the best intentions, succumb to the spotlight and do all the talking. Ego, insecurity or lack of trust in subordinates may cause this to happen. When you script the calls with your manager, you can attempt to establish your role, bearing in mind that it may change in front of the customer.

While scheduling calls with your manager, you should discuss what kind of a briefing he or she desires. The extent of the briefing depends on individual style and familiarity with the account. It may be as simple as a copy of the last credit write-up and profitability data or it may be an extensive memo.

Anyone accompanying you on a call needs enough information to be effective. The further removed they are from the customer, for example, senior management, the more information they need. If senior management is active in calling efforts, your organization may have standardized briefings for account calls. More likely, each briefing will take a form of its own. Try to put yourself in the shoes of the recipient and think what will enhance effectiveness. Your briefing might include a description of the company, extent and profitability of the relationship, competitive position, information about management, objectives of the call, specific role of the recipient of the briefing, and so forth. These briefings are important because they reflect how you analyze the relationship. They will be remembered.

SCRIPTING

Whether you are alone or accompanied by your manager and the previous account officer, every call should be carefully scripted in advance. The manager should establish this behavior as part of the sales management process, but you are responsible for ensuring that your calls are scripted.

Successful bankers do not "wing it." They carefully plan and script their behaviors with customers. Much of their spontaneity is actually rehearsed. They are always flexible enough to change course should conditions dictate it. However, they normally accomplish the objectives they establish.

In your call preparation, you should have set forth three to five objectives you wish to accomplish on the call. These should be quite straightforward, for example:

1. Establish your authority as the new account officer and alert the owner that you will call for another appointment.
2. Determine if the credit facilities you have extended are adequate for the coming year.
3. Qualify the account for an additional service.
4. Understand the reasons for the loss last quarter and the outlook for the future.

Your scripting with others on the call should be done in the office and reviewed in the car, or done in the car, in the parking lot, or in the elevator, but scripting should always be done before arrival. At a minimum you should script the:

- *Opening remarks.* Designate who starts the discussion and what will be said. For example, the previous account officer makes the introductions and then the manager establishes your authority and suggests a plant tour followed by a brief meeting back in the office to review a few issues.

Scripting openings avoids pregnant pauses or everyone blurting out different topics at once.

- *Plant tour*. Do you tour the facilities or save that for a time when you are alone and can do it in great detail? You should always call at the place of business of the customer and whenever possible, tour the facilities, so you can relate them to the financial statements.
- *Objectives*. Establish who is responsible for the accomplishment of objectives. For example, you talk about the adequacy of the credit line, the previous account officer qualifies the customer for a remote disbursement account, and the manager examines the loss for the quarter. Obviously, there should be a free flowing dialogue with everyone participating. But the previous account officer is cued to bring up the remote disbursement account once you have obtained the information on the adequacy of the line.
- *Departure time*. Agree on a time by which you will leave the customer. This discipline keeps you on schedule and focuses the discussions.

Things rarely go exactly as scripted, and you should be prepared for a change in course. Never be so overscripted that you miss the subtle signals that the customer has a different agenda. Nevertheless, scripting is an easy but powerful tool to maximize the effectiveness of your calling efforts.

MEETING THE CUSTOMER

With all the research, planning, and prioritizing you have done, actually meeting the customer may seem anticlimactic. However, the introductory call is just the beginning of a long journey. Assuming your organization believes in relationship banking, you will have at least three long-term objectives to accomplish beyond the limited goals of your first call.

First, you will want to establish a rapport with the customer that through mutual respect leads to a partnership rather than a vendor relationship. You want to be at the customer's planning table as a trusted advisor like a good accountant or lawyer. If you cannot add value to the relationship through your professionalism, your products become commodities, and you can only compete on price or structure.

Second, you need to develop an intimate understanding of the risks involved in extending credit to the customer. This understanding entails more than financial statement analysis. You must know the customer's market and industry. You also must know how management thinks and operates and how it might react to a changing environment.

Third, you must know the customer in-depth to be able to recognize and sell your bank's products and services. Given the current overcapacity in the banking industry, a commercial loan by itself is rarely profitable. You will need to cross-sell other products and services to cement the relationship and make it profitable in the long run.

In your introductory call and in future calls to develop the relationship, there are a number of skills you should begin to master. Be aware of these skills and do some periodic self-assessment. Also, observe others and adapt what they do best.

STYLES

People have many different personality styles. Once you are able to recognize some of them, you may, on occasion, wish to adapt your approach to different styles. However, the real issue is the recognition of differences. Never make sweeping assumptions, such as only an extrovert can run a sales-oriented company. To gain some insights into personality differences, you should complete some of the personality inventory instruments available through your human resources department. No style is good or bad, but understanding yourself better is a start to understanding the differences of others.

Age differences can raise real or perceived problems. As a new account officer, you may be decades younger than some of your customers. The best way to overcome this problem is through professionalism. Make sure every call is well planned with an agenda that adds value. You must demonstrate that you can deliver the resources of the bank and that you have significant support within the organization. Never refer to a loan committee or some other body that makes decisions. If you do, the customer will want to talk to the loan committee rather than a person running errands for it.

If you sense discomfort over age differences, occasionally schedule a call including a senior member of your organization. Also, get a sense of succession within your customer's company and cultivate relationships with the next generation. You should ensure that your organization is developing relationships at all levels of the company. For example, it may make sense to have someone in your operations department know the controller of your customer. You want your organization and your customer to be able to resolve issues without elevating each problem to the president or to you.

INTERVIEWING

An interview with a customer or prospect should have a natural flow rather than the artificiality often produced by a checklist of questions. When novices use a questionnaire, they are often so focused on formulating the next question that they do not hear what the customer says. This inattention soon becomes apparent and annoying to the customer.

The trick to a successful interview is to ensure that the customer does most of the talking while being gently guided into revealing the information you need. Since your customer is talking, your listening skills become as important as your questioning technique. Listening is not a passive skill. It requires concentration, note-taking, and the body language that indicates you really are listening. Taking notes is particularly helpful. Note-taking not only helps you remember information but it also signals to the customer that you are listening.

If you cannot use a checklist to make sure you get all the information you need, what can you do? One technique is to use a financial statement as an interviewing questionnaire. In the case of a customer, you have the company's financial statements. With a prospect, you may need to imagine them. For example, you have done enough financial analysis to conjure up these mental images, which raise issues such as the following:

Balance Sheet

Cash	Accounts payable
Accounts receivable	Notes payable
Inventory	Long-term debt
Equipment, land, and buildings	Equity

Income Statement

Sales

Cost of goods sold

Gross profit

Selling, general, and administrative expenses

Taxes

Net profit

- Cash—current bank relations, mixture of currency and checks, deposit and disbursement procedures, cash management practices.

- Accounts receivable—major customers, concentrations, credit terms, turnover, credit policies, bad-debt experience, reserves.
- Inventory—accounting methodology, controls, obsolescence, turnover, storage capacity, shipping procedures, availability.
- Equipment, land, and buildings—ownership, condition, adequacy, market versus book value, maintenance costs, purchase decision process, financing, future acquisitions.
- Accounts payable—principal vendors, payment terms, special dating, alternative supplies.
- Notes payable—short-term financing philosophy, creditors, terms, security interests.
- Long-term debt—creditors, collateral, terms, match to cash flows.
- Equity—ownership, board of directors, decision-making process, dividend policy, history.
- Sales—market and industry conditions, competitors, trends, pricing, volatility.
- Cost of goods sold—margin stability, volume versus pricing constraints, break-even points.
- Selling, general, and administrative expenses—number of employees, union representation, relations, sales force.
- Taxes—C or S corporation, withholding current, last tax audit.

Open-ended questions force an explanation or amplification rather than a simple yes or no. Have some useful open-ended questions at the ready, for example:

- "What is your company going to look like in five years?" The answer may demonstrate the planning ability or vision of the owner. Occasionally, you may hear something startling such as a sale of the company or a completely new direction in strategy.
- "What are some of the things you worry about in running your company?" The answer may indicate contingency planning ability and point out areas that should concern you.
- "At the end of your year, what do you consider good performance?" The answer may illustrate the focus of management. For example, you may think that cash generation is job number one, while management is thinking in terms of sales volume.

- "How much risk are you willing to take to achieve your performance objectives?" The answer may give you an idea of the risk tolerance of management, but you may need to do some probing or clarifying. For example, amplify by asking about entry into new markets, comfort with higher debt levels, and so forth.

Other useful tools to develop rapport along with credit and sales knowledge are the financial spreads and data routinely produced in your own bank. It is amazing how much financial analysis is produced and used internally and then buried in credit files without showing it to and discussing it with customers. Even accountants who prepare financial statements for customers rarely discuss or interpret them. They usually focus on the tax implications.

A useful annual call might include giving the customer a copy of the spreadsheets with areas of discussion highlighted. Pointing out positive and negative trends and areas of concern or consideration can be valuable for your customer and demonstrate your professionalism.

Plant Tours

Touring the facilities gives you a better idea of the customer's operations and is usually enjoyable. A tour can demonstrate where management is focusing efforts and allow management to discuss concerns. It also gives you information not available in the financial statements, such as the condition of plant and equipment, capacity issues, internal controls, environmental concerns, and the quality of the labor force. You should relate what you see to the financial statements and examine any unexplained differences.

Generally, the plant tour is not a good opportunity for talking about business. In many manufacturing operations, you are lucky to hear a word that is spoken. Also, you want to follow management's lead and see what they consider important.

Setting Expectations

Over time, you want to establish mutual expectations with your customers, particularly new customers. Setting expectations can prevent problems and help preserve relationships.

Your customers should expect that you can deliver the bank's resources, provided requests are reasonable and within policy limitations. Explaining a bank's loan policy is not always easy, especially if you are inexperienced. When in doubt, seek clarification from your manager. Articulating loan policy is a responsibility of management.

A customer can expect that you can deliver the bank, explain the ground rules, and provide timely responses. Nothing is more damaging than a protracted "maybe." Your customer also expects that you learn his or her business and add value to the relationship.

You can expect that the customer include you at the planning table and that there will be no surprises. You want to be informed immediately of losses or other bad news. You should expect no overdrafts, which are a sign of sloppiness and bad planning. You should expect the timely submission of financial data and other mutually agreed-on information. Although you understand and appreciate the competitive environment, you expect to be given a first opportunity to submit proposals on new requests and these proposals will not be used to shop the competition.

As with any relationship, the key is honesty, open communications, and an understanding of mutual expectations. Without them, you are a mere vendor on a list and will receive the occasional bid request. Some customers only want a vendor relationship, and there may be little you can do to change that attitude. However, you should change your approach to that customer.

DEBRIEFING

After completing the customer call, the travel time back to the office provides an excellent opportunity to debrief and gain feedback. You should review the objectives for the call and determine if they have been accomplished. If not, why not?

If your manager does not fall easily into coaching and counseling, you might pose questions such as:

- How do you think the call went?
- Do you have any suggestions for improving my interviewing techniques?
- Would you have changed any of the ways we handled this call?
- Do you have any suggestions for my calls on this customer in the future?
- What was your strategy in asking about the role of the board in approving capital expenditures?

Immediately following a call, you will find it helpful to make written notes of any information you want to retain or act on. If you are making a series of calls, remembering important information and to which customer it pertains can be quite a challenge by the end of the day.

To help establish that you are the new account officer, you may wish to send the customer a thank-you note with your business card. This note puts your name before the customer once again and assists the transition. Be sure to follow up promptly on any issues developed during the call.

If you made the call yourself, then debrief yourself and review the call objectives against results. By now, you should be well into the disciplines of self-management.

SUMMARY

Meeting and dealing with your customer base should be exciting. Call preparation including basic research and discussions with team members and your manager can produce substantial benefit. You should never "wing it." A call on a customer should be carefully scripted with a limited number of specific objectives. However, you should also bear in mind longer term objectives of building rapport and understanding risks and sales opportunities. Accomplishing your goal requires learning, practicing, and perfecting interviewing and other skills and techniques.

Chapter 3

Marketing

Now that you have met your customer base and, in subsequent calls, have begun developing rapport and a sense of credit and sales opportunities, it is time to begin working on marketing skills. If your organization has a strong marketing and sales culture, developing your own skills is relatively easy. If such a culture is lacking, you must rely much more on your self-management disciplines.

THE SALES CULTURE

To begin, you must assess the quality of the sales culture, so you can fill in any gaps on your own. This process ultimately makes you a much better manager, should your career path lead in that direction.

How can you recognize a strong sales culture? There are a number of tangible indicators of a sales culture that do not take long to assess. Consistency is a key feature of a strong sales culture, so when examining the indicators, determine whether they are "one-shot" events or part of the fabric of doing business.

SALES TRAINING

Consultative selling is an honorable and ethical approach of communicating with a customer or prospect, discovering needs, and fulfilling them in a mutually profitable manner. It is truly a "win-win" arrangement in which everyone benefits. The approach requires a knowledge of your organization's products, an understanding of your customer's needs, selling skills, and constant training and reinforcement.

Discovering and understanding the needs of a customer and then selling a solution cannot be considered a natural behavior. We tend to see things through our own eyes rather than someone else's. Sales training asks you to put yourself in the place of the customer and then covers a number of techniques including openings, needs identification, qualifying, product features, objections, and closings.

In a strong sales culture, you should receive basic sales training followed periodically by more advanced skill training. Your manager should reinforce these skills at periodic sales meetings.

PRODUCT TRAINING

Most banks offer a bewildering array of products because new products are in constant development and old products are rarely pruned. In a strong sales culture, managers know which products make sense in their marketplace and which are the most profitable.

Consequently, the number of products that a commercial banker is expected to sell is reduced to a manageable number of the most profitable products. Product managers often look at commercial bankers as unpaid salespersons and ask them to push all sorts of unprofitable creations. A good sales manager protects the turf and marketplace ensuring that the products to be sold are manageable and profitable and that they work.

With a reasonable number of products, commercial bankers can receive focused product training that is sales oriented rather than technically oriented. Bankers learn features, qualifying criteria, objections, competitive position, and pricing as opposed to information in a user's manual.

The manager also trains bankers in the appropriate time to hand the customer off to a specialist. When the specialist or technician steps in, the banker must decide if his or her continued presence is adding value. If it is not, it is time to move on to the next sale.

STANDARDS

Standards are the minimum expectations or the minimum levels of acceptable performance for commercial bankers. If you were to perform at the level set by all standards, you would be performing adequately but not exceptionally. Standards detail acceptable levels of activities, workloads, and results. In a strong sales culture, the standards cover both sales and credit results because, in successful organizations, credit and sales are merged into one culture and policy.

A list of standards might include:

- Number of borrowing customers.
- Total commitments and outstandings.
- Maximum documentation and credit exceptions.

- Number of nonborrowing customers.
- Number of active prospects.
- Number and amount of demand and time deposits.
- Amount of fee income generated.
- Net profit after tax generated by the banker.
- Maximum past-due percentage.
- Maximum watch-list percentage.
- Number of annual customer calls.
- Number of annual prospect calls.
- Number of significant new relationships added annually.
- Number of referrals to other departments.
- Customer satisfaction minimums.

Standards are not objectives. Periodically, and at least annually, your manager will discuss and establish specific objectives with you. These objectives focus on behaviors that need to be improved or areas that management is emphasizing. Good managers follow up on these objectives, usually by requesting a report from you, at least on a quarterly basis.

MARKETING

In a strong sales culture, management and the commercial banking staff have a good idea of market share and trends, product penetration of the customer base or wallet share, customer profitability, product costs, and customer satisfaction. Very few commercial banks can currently state that they have mastered these marketing requirements. Nevertheless, progressive organizations are realizing that fundamental marketing skills are necessary to survival.

Although banks are rapidly losing market share to nonbank competition, they have one untapped advantage that will be the salvation of the shrewdest. Banks are somewhat unwittingly sitting on the mother lode of customer information. Stashed away in credit files and electronic impulses is the most current and complete data obtainable on consumer and corporate assets, liabilities, cash flows, payment habits, investment choices, and demographic material. Smart bankers are learning to mine this information and use it as a powerful marketing tool. Imagine what the top mutual funds or brokerage firms would do if they had access to this information.

In assessing your organization's marketing skills you might start with determining if anyone knows what your share of the market is and if it is trending up or down. You may be disappointed. Banking was once a highly regulated industry with proscribed markets, so strong marketing skills were not that important. Banking does not have the marketing history of, say, a consumer products company.

In fairness, market share is not an easy concept in banking. If you are selling cars, every vehicle sold is registered, so market share is not difficult to compute. In commercial banking, you might, with some difficulty, be able to develop share data from call reports of your immediate competitors, but you would be hard pressed to gauge what the nonbank competition is taking.

If you are selling soap, you are not concerned with income-to-debt ratios or whether the buyer is of good character or a serial killer. In commercial banking, you must define the parameters of your target company in a given market and then qualify them to determine your potential market. This process is expensive and time-consuming.

In larger markets, such as big metropolitan areas, markets may be divided into segments with a manager responsible for each geographical segment. In smaller markets, one commercial banking manager may be responsible for the entire market. The challenges are the same. The manager must profile the target customer to differentiate it from a target of another banking unit such as small business, retail, or national accounts. The profile might focus on sales size, number of employees, or potential borrowing needs.

Once profiled, the manager lists the targets in the market area and, over time, qualifies them as prospects. The number of customers within the qualified target base is one way to measure market share. Then the manager assigns prospects to the sale force and monitors results.

The manager also is concerned with wallet share or how effectively a wide range of products has been sold to customers that qualify for them. If profitable products are not being sold, product training may be indicated.

The following two reports, Exhibits 3.1 and 3.2, illustrate different levels of sophistication and perhaps understanding of a market. Although Exhibit 3.1 is definitely preferable, Exhibit 3.2 is better than nothing and is a good base on which to improve.

Exhibit 3.2 is a less sophisticated report that is, nevertheless, a good starting point in market development. It assumes the reader knows the definition of the market area, the target profile, and the qualifying standards. Only businesses that fit the profile and qualification standards are listed and then the

EXHIBIT 3.1

COMMERCIAL BANKING MARKETING PLAN

The geographic area for which the commercial banking department is responsible is Parkerson County. As this territory has been defined for four years, we are reasonably confident that we have identified all the commercial businesses within our boundaries. We profile a target commercial business as one with annual sales of $2-$50 million, 10 or more employees, and potential borrowing needs of at least $250,000. Of a total of 310 businesses, we have qualified 215 or 69% as potentially meeting our loan policy. This is a net decrease of 10 businesses or 5% from last year. The net decrease of 10 businesses is made up of 4 new prospects less 12 deleted prospects and 3 new customers less 5 ex-customers. We sense that the geographic area is in a slow decline because of mergers and the lack of new businesses owing to unfavorable tax considerations.

Of the 215 total qualified businesses, 139, or 65%, are our customers. We define a customer as a business that has executed a certificate of authority and has at least one product from us. Our share of the market of 65% is up from 62% last year. Our data are not accurate enough for comparisons from prior years.

Attachment A is a list of our prospects and customers by responsible officer. The prospects are listed in priority order, and the customers are listed in descending order of profitability.

We have analyzed all our customers for products and services that they are using or could reasonably use. The attachment B illustrates our wallet share by product. Wallet share is defined as the percentage of customers using a given product divided by the number of customers qualified for that product.

Next year, we feel we can add a net of 4 customers, increasing our market share to 67%. We can increase wallet share in remote disbursements and 401K plans. To accomplish the increase, staff members are attending additional product training. Training will be completed in two months.

Attachment C is a list of out-of-territory accounts and the rationale for maintaining them. Attachment D is relationship plans on our top 10 prospects and customers.

Given our minimum standards, we feel we are adequately staffed, but we could become overstaffed if our market continues to deteriorate.

To accomplish our plan, we will need an additional $5,000 for product and sales training and the willingness of senior management to be involved in 10 prospect solicitations and 10 customer calls.

EXHIBIT 3.2

QUALIFIED COMMERCIAL BUSINESSES IN OUR MARKET

Business Name	Primary Account Relationship	Secondary Account Relationship	Nominal Account Relationship	No Relationship

type of relationship is checked. Totals and percentages are then calculated and followed over time.

In its most simplified terms, marketing is the effective management of lists. Developing the lists is time-consuming and costly, but it focuses sales efforts and maximizes results. Banks can no longer afford to have their sales forces wandering around markets in random patterns.

SALES MANAGEMENT

Using the market data developed through great effort and expense, the manager can make intelligent customer and prospect assignments and monitor results through short but frequent sales meetings designed to change behavior. Most people do not want to sell. It is not a natural behavior because people fear rejection and failure.

You can expect your manager to hold a brief sales meeting on Monday at which goals and deadlines are established. During the week, he or she should check on progress and offer coaching and counseling. On Friday, there may be a quick debriefing meeting to check on progress of the entire group. The good sales manager leaves nothing to chance.

QUALITY AND CUSTOMER SATISFACTION

Sometimes quality is treated like a fad, which is briefly endorsed and then forgotten in favor of whatever comes next. Nevertheless, quality and customer satisfaction are vital to your success. Customer satisfaction is closely related to quality and can be measured in commercial banking through periodic customer surveys. The levels and trends of customer satisfaction should become a part of performance evaluation.

CREDIT AND SALES

Historically, credit policy and marketing and sales policies were made in isolation. Consequently, there were cyclical periods of emphasis on sales that resulted in bad credit decisions. Then there would be a cleanup period in which credit was emphasized and marketing deteriorated. The unfortunate result was wildly fluctuating earnings or worse and low stock valuations compared with broader markets.

Intelligent bankers now see that credit and sales are two sides of the same coin and are now merging them into one integrated policy and culture. Qualifying prospects assumes that credit and sales are merged. A well-managed, aggressive sales force is critical to credit success. A good banker would rather look at 10 transactions and do 3 of them than look at 3 and do 3. Approximately 5-10% of most commercial loan portfolios must be pruned every year because of deteriorating borrowers. The willingness to prune in a timely fashion improves significantly if an aggressive sales effort produces a full pipeline of business ready to replace the pruned accounts.

INDICATORS

The foregoing description of a strong marketing and sales culture is intended to give you a point of reference so that you can assess your own environment. A brief checklist of indicators of a strong sales culture may also be helpful:

- *Common terminology*. Does everyone know and use common terms, such as scripting, pipeline, qualified prospect?
- *Markets*. Are target markets, profiled targets, qualified targets, market share, customer penetration adequately defined?
- *Customer profitability*. Do you have a profitability system that accounts for all customer's relationships with reasonable allocations and accurate costs?
- *Sales management*. Is there a sales management process with periodic meetings to monitor and encourage progress?
- *Training*. Does everyone receive periodic sales and product training?
- *Quality*. Can you measure and are you held accountable for quality and customer satisfaction?
- *Management*. Is senior management consistently involved in the sales process?

SELF MANAGEMENT

Now that you have some idea of what a strong marketing culture looks like, you can assess your own environment and determine the shortfalls that you must overcome through your own efforts.

Do not rely on your organization's marketing department. Most bank marketing departments lack a clear mission and compare unfavorably with marketing departments in other financial institutions such as mutual funds and brokerage firms. Your marketing department is probably consumer-oriented and saddled with miscellaneous projects and events that are time-consuming but produce little for the bottom line.

If you do not have a strong sales manager, the situation is far from hopeless. By identifying organizational shortfalls, you can accomplish much on your own and perhaps elevate the state of the art in the process.

SALES TRAINING

Selling is an art form with particular skills that must be mastered through repetition. Because selling focuses on the customer rather than on self, it is not natural behavior. Therefore, it is difficult to learn without help.

If your organization does not routinely provide sales training, ask for it. The best training is generally provided by an outside consultant to all members of the team and the manager. The training teaches the elements of selling, reinforcing them through role playing and videotaped exercises. The manager also should receive additional sales management training. When training is delivered in a team environment, expectations are established for everyone, and the manager can provide follow-up, coaching, and counseling. Periodically, more advanced team training should be given for such skills as negotiating, listening, and interviewing.

If team training is unavailable, then find the better books among the many that have been published. Do your own research if no one can recommend any. If you must rely on books, use what you have learned when you script a call and then critique yourself afterwards.

Talk to salespeople in other industries such as insurance and brokerage about how they were trained and what obstacles they encountered. Also, watch some of the better performers in your organization and question them about their techniques. Most will be delighted to help.

PRODUCT KNOWLEDGE

Examine your most profitable customers and determine why they are profitable. You will probably notice that they are not only loan customers but also heavy users of several products and services.

To enhance your own product knowledge, select a manageable number of products to start, say three to five, and confirm your choices with your manager. You will want to ensure that your bank can deliver these products efficiently and competitively and that they are well supported internally. Unfortunately, you will find that some products just do not work very well or are unprofitable, but no one seems willing to discard them.

You can develop product knowledge by talking to specialists, going on a call at which the product is being sold, and reviewing bank materials. Focus on the selling aspects of the products rather than technical data. Some of the product information you must develop includes:

- A layperson's description of what the product does.
- Benefits offered to a potential customer.
- The target market and who qualifies for the product. Obtain a representative list of customers and a case history.
- Probing questions to determine need along with potential objections and responses.
- Pricing and competitive position.
- The implementation process.
- Closing requirements such as contracts.

If you are ultimately expected to sell 10 to 20 products, doing your own product knowledge research is inefficient. An alert manager standardizes the learning process.

STANDARDS

If your unit does not have standards setting minimum expectations, then set your own. It may take some creativity and periodic reassessment and resetting. Even though you may just be getting started as a commercial banker, set your standards at what you think they should be for a reasonably experienced banker. No one expects you to perform at standard on day one. Much depends on what type of a portfolio, if any, you inherit.

You can gain insights concerning appropriate workload standards by talking to your peers and examining data such as the trial balance from your commercial loan system. What co-workers are doing is not necessarily right, but it is a good starting point.

Establishing marketing standards requires a fairly thorough understanding of your marketplace. Part of your challenge is determining how much time to spend on your customer base and how much on prospects. Generally, your customer base is a more fertile ground for immediate sales. However, in most portfolios, 5-10% of customers deteriorate annually and must be pruned and replaced.

With constant pruning, you must have an active sales effort to produce a pipeline of new customers. In a market that is stagnant or growing at the gross domestic product level and amply competitive, it should take you two to three years to convert a prospect into a customer. The prospect you want is an excellent customer of a competitor and should not switch easily. Beware of the prospect that moves too easily. Your best sales are the hardest to achieve.

In determining your customer-to-prospect calling mix, you should examine the wallet share or product penetration of existing customers. If wallet share is low, put more weight on customer calls without ignoring, however, your prospects. Marketing is truly an art, and you should discuss your approach with your manager and peers.

Credit standards are vital counterbalances to excessive exuberance on the sales side. In a strong culture, credit and sales are merged into one operating philosophy. To balance sales standards, you also should establish credit standards, such as maximum documentation and administrative exceptions, watch-listed credits, past-due payments, nonaccruals, and charge-offs. Your loan review department should be helpful in suggesting standards.

Unfortunately, many banks focus solely on such data as past-due payments, nonaccruals, and charge-offs, which is like timing your cooking with a smoke detector. By the time accounts fall that far, it is often too late to make corrections. You should instead, focus your attention on the watch list, which contains your credit destiny.

Setting a standard for the maximum amount of watch-listed credits you can carry requires examining your bank's credit history through business cycles. Ideally, your bank should be performing a migration analysis, that is, tracking pools of similarly risk rated loans over time to discover their various outcomes. If your bank does not keep or track such data, you might make an educated guess after discussion with your manager and loan review. Most commercial loan portfolios cannot carry a watch list in excess of 10% of outstandings and still hit their profitability targets over time.

Once you develop your standards, discuss them with your manager and resolve any areas of discomfort or disagreement. The discussion should help clarify expectations and remove some of the ambiguity that you are facing.

MARKETING

While setting standards, you considered the proportion of prospect-to-customer calls you should be making. This knowledge is helpful in developing your prospect list. The list combines internally developed prospects with leads you initiate on your own. The stronger the marketing culture, the easier it is to develop a good prospect list.

Prioritize your list, and focus your efforts on a manageable portion. The remainder of the list is for replenishment of your active prospects. As you work on your active prospects, your efforts should lead toward making proposals for the sale of products. As proposals are presented, add them to your sales pipeline report. A pipeline report attempts to manage and predict the amount of new business that might be achieved with a given period of time, say, six months. The report lists prospects or customers where proposals have been made and a percentage probability of landing them.

You should periodically discuss your prospect list with your manager and peers. Not only can you receive helpful advice but you also may be unaware of hidden issues or credit problems. Ideally, active prospects should be prescreened for credit, so you do not waste time on fruitless calling efforts.

CONFLICTS AND CHALLENGES

You can help your manager immeasurably, and yourself in the process, by developing self-management skills and discussing them with your manager. For example, developing your own standards if none exist is a relatively painless method of setting expectations with your manager. Most managers will welcome such initiatives because it assists them in doing their job. Nevertheless, you may encounter issues that are not so easy to resolve.

THE BUDGET

Although banking is a cyclical business, management tends to straight-line budgets upward as if the business cycle never existed. Results have been highly cyclical despite straight-line budgets because of periodic credit crashes. Straight-line budgets depend on increased loan volume unless management has diversified the revenues of the organization. Consequently, managers find themselves under constant pressure to increase volume in stagnant and competitive marketplaces.

The best antidote to this mindless pressure on volume is a strong marketing culture in which management truly understands the realities and potential of a given market. A strong credit culture demands an equally strong marketing and sales culture. If your organization does not have such a culture, you may feel significant pressures and face conflicts that are difficult to resolve.

SALES CYCLE

If your manager is feeling pressure on the volume front, you may receive signals to speed up the sales cycle. The easiest way to do this is to go down market in credit quality or loosen pricing and credit structuring standards.

Of course, few managers will say outright that it is time to reduce credit standards and trash the organization's pricing and structure. Many managers do so unwittingly as they receive encouragement from management and watch their competitors lower standards. Staying the course requires a great deal of courage. Commercial lending is a tempting environment for denial because the results of reduced standards will not appear for several years.

THE SIGNALS

The signals to reduce standards usually come in the tangible forms of promotion, recognition, and rewards, and the intangible in the forms of body language and encouragement. Most managers are unaware of the signals they are emitting, but they are being constantly received and interpreted by line bankers. These signals often directly contradict the official party line and, therefore, create conflict and frustration.

As a novice commercial lender, you are not going to change the tide of events in an organization lowering standards. That is a management responsibility. Nevertheless, when you recognize and feel the conflict, you should discuss it with your manager, peers, and a trusted mentor in an attempt to resolve it in your own mind.

SUMMARY

To develop your own marketing skills, you must be able to recognize the components of a strong marketing and sales culture. You should then compare that culture with the one you are experiencing and determine if there are any gaps. These gaps should be filled in with self-management disciplines.

If the gaps are significant, you might find it necessary to obtain your own sales and product training, establish standards, and develop a marketing plan. Discuss these efforts with your manager to set mutual expectations and resolve conflicts. You will help your manager, and yourself, in the process.

By now, you have discovered that success in commercial banking requires mastering self-management disciplines and making them instinctive and lifelong habits. With these basic disciplines in place, you can focus on the flawless and consistent execution of fundamental skills. As obvious as this course of action may be, it is not widely practiced. Self-management disciplines and the consistent execution of fundamentals gives you a massive competitive advantage and makes commercial banking rewarding and enjoyable.

Chapter 4

Examining the Loan Request

Your first loan request does not come to you as a nicely packaged case study with appendices containing financial spreads and market and industry analyses. Using your interviewing skills and research, you must develop the request so that it meets the customer's needs while fitting your loan policy. Loan policies are often ambiguous and customers can be demanding, so responding to a loan request tests your negotiating skills both with the borrower and in your organization.

As you develop the loan proposal, you should prepare it to fit into the loan administration process of your organization. A brief review of the process follows.

COMMERCIAL LOAN ADMINISTRATION

Commercial loan administration is a logical, sequential process of administering individual loans so that the portfolio as a whole accomplishes planned objectives. There are five distinct phases of loan administration and you must understand how they affect you and your customers.

1. Loan Policy

At its best, loan policy is an agreement among management, credit, and the line on what is to be accomplished with a given marketplace. It addresses the mission, target markets, types of desired customers, concentration limits, performance expectations, underwriting standards, and loan authorities. It merges credit, marketing, and sales objectives into one policy.

Loan policies for specialized markets such as real estate, auto dealers, cattle feeding, and so forth can be quite specific, whereas policies for the general business market are fairly generic. It is impossible to write policy that covers every conceivable commercial business. Consequently, much policy in this area is unwritten and is guided by experience and common sense.

Although new commercial bankers can understand why everything cannot be captured in a policy document, the unwritten policy is frustrating, nevertheless. How do you know what is a good deal for the bank? An understanding manager overcomes this problem by having as many open discussions about credits as possible. Some forum, such as a weekly departmental credit meeting, can be beneficial. Here, credits can be discussed in an informal and nonthreatening manner before the loan approval stage. This process not only is educational but also uses the collective experience to advantage. Also, each manager has credit biases that may not be reflected in the bank's loan policy. If your manager was once burned on a contractor loan, you should know about it because that incident will affect your department's loan policy.

Discuss credit opportunities in the early stage with your manager and peers. These discussions are not a sign of weakness. Rather, they should be viewed as a way to accelerate learning, improve efficiency, and avoid embarrassment with customers. The good manager considers this time well spent.

2. Loan Approval

Loan approval is a process that tests individual transactions against the screen of loan policy and approves, modifies, or rejects them. If the loan policy is well understood and communicated, rejection is a fairly rare occurrence.

A good loan approval process also provides shared experiences, training, communications, and enhancement of the credit culture. As such, you exercise your listening skills as much as your persuasive skills. As a new commercial banker, you naturally want to make your mark by adding profitable loans to the portfolio. However, pushing the boundaries of approval makes little sense until you have a thorough understanding of loan policy and risk and reward and some experience with problem credits. Gaining this understanding and experience usually takes a full business cycle, and by then, you may not be so eager to push the edges of policy.

3. Monitoring

When a loan is approved and booked, it is given a risk rating that places it in a segment of the portfolio with other loans of similar risk. The manager of the portfolio monitors these segments of risk, among other indicators, to ensure the portfolio meets objectives.

After you book the loan, it is your responsibility to assist the manager by ensuring that the initial risk rating is correct and that you change it in a timely manner when conditions warrant. Remain alert to changes in risk by establishing a monitoring process with your borrower that is reviewed in the loan approval process.

Loan monitoring is expensive, so it should focus on the minimum needed to detect changes in risk. The customer should be involved in the process and, in fact, should do most of the work by giving you periodic compliance certificates. When a violation occurs, it warrants immediate attention, starting with alerting your manager.

Your manager does not want to be surprised, nor does he or she want to be asked by the next level of management about something that you have failed to bring to his or her attention. Surprises do happen, and occasionally, they appear in the newspaper. When that occurs, brief your manager quickly before being asked and then determine if anyone else should be informed.

4. Loan Review

Loan review is an objective, third-party review of the portfolio as a whole. It should draw conclusions on risk-rating reliability, reserves, trends, management, and if the portfolio is meeting objectives. When due diligence is conducted in acquisitions, it establishes what the acquirer should be willing to pay for the portfolio. Loan review internally should be conducted with the same intensity of purpose.

New commercial bankers often feel they are being personally attacked by loan review when their portfolios are audited. The loan review process is another time when it pays to listen as much as to persuade. Loan review is an institutionalized process of conveying objective, professional feedback. Take advantage of it.

5. Problem Loans

Most commercial loan portfolios experience, on average, a 5-10% annual deterioration to the watch list and a 0.5% net charge-off ratio. Individual bank experience will vary with different loan policies, quality of management, and local economic and competitive conditions. However, problem loans are a fact of life in any portfolio, so your bank should have a well-rehearsed problem loan drill.

In consumer loan portfolios, a problem loan is a statistic. In commercial loan portfolios, many insecure or novice lenders consider a problem loan a blot on their escutcheons. Having a problem credit is not a sin. In fact, it is statistically inevitable. The real sin is denying the problem and failing to react to it. If you believe you have a problem credit, your duty is to discuss it immediately with your manager. Your manager is responsible for creating an environment in which early discussion of problems is encouraged and rewarded.

You detect problems through financial and nonfinancial signals and covenant violations. When you detect a problem, discuss it immediately with your manager. Be prepared to recommend a risk-rating change and a course of action with the customer. If the customer's risk rating is still acceptable and the outlook is reasonably encouraging, you may recommend additional collateral, higher pricing, and a renegotiation of the covenants.

As part of your bank's problem loan drill, your manager should designate some segment of the risk-rating spectrum as a decision point for exiting or maintaining the customer. This decision point should be one step away from the watch list so the customer is still attractive to another institution but exhibiting trends that if not reversed, will lead to a watch-listed credit.

Because this decision point is judgmental, you should not hesitate to discuss potential problems with your manager. But before approaching your manager, decide if you want to maintain or exit the customer and develop your recommendation. A maintain decision should be based on the following criteria:

- The borrower understands there is a problem and is willing to do something about it. Borrowers often have their egos involved in the business, and denial can be your worst problem.
- The borrower has an action plan, with which you agree, for dealing with the problem. You may have guided or coaxed the borrower into developing a plan, but the plan is the borrower's and not yours.
- The borrower has a contingency plan in case the action plan fails and has designated a point at which failure is acknowledged. The contingency plan may be liquidation of the business. Again, it must be the borrower's plan and not yours. If unpleasant steps must be taken, make sure it is the borrower that sets the course of action.
- The borrower is willing to commit additional resources in collateral, guaranties, or equity.
- The borrower is willing to accept repricing of the credit to reflect the new risks involved.

An exit decision is best made while the credit is still attractive to some other institution. It is a difficult decision because once it moves, you will probably wonder if you were too hasty. Unfortunately, the only way to find out is to delay the decision to the point at which it might be too late and you have a workout on your hands. If you have an aggressive sales effort producing a constant pipeline of new business, your decision will be much easier.

THE LOAN DECISION

When you examine a loan request, you are preparing for all areas of administration. You must decide whether the request meets your loan policy and, if not, can it be modified through negotiation to comply. If you feel it complies, you must prepare for your loan approval process, including deciding how you intend to monitor the borrower. Monitoring should ensure risk-rating accuracy and continued compliance with loan policy, which will be periodically verified by loan review. In the event your borrower deteriorates, your documentation should give you the right to act, and you should have prepared a second way out with collateral or guaranties.

It helps to break all these tasks down into manageable components. There are seven elements of a loan decision, and each element raises questions that you must be prepared to answer. You develop these answers through interviews and negotiations, analysis of financial statements and other materials, and calling on your own experience and intuition. The seven elements follow.

1. EXAMINING THE BORROWER

You analyze the borrower on three different planes—management, environment, and financial structure. Although it is convenient to segment these components, never forget that they are interrelated. Financial structure and results are a function of management decisions made in a competitive environment. The ability to understand, describe, and draw conclusions from these relationships is what distinguishes a good analyst from a mediocre one.

While perhaps the most critical component of a credit decision, your view of management is highly judgmental. Therefore, be cautious about what you put in a file subject to subpoena. You should develop a view on the following issues:

- *Character*. Unfortunately, you can never fully understand character until it is tested. Prestige and social standing have nothing to do with it. How someone reacted to adversity in the past is a good indicator. Life-style and the handling of personal debt is another. Use your common sense.
- *Ability*. Track record is a good indicator, but the loan you are making now will be repaid in the future. The real issue is, Can management recognize and adapt to change? Contingency planning is one indicator.
- *Depth*. Are you dependent on one individual, and can you mitigate this risk through disability and life insurance? Succession, particularly in family owned businesses, is a complex issue that you must address.

- *Vision*. Does management know where it wants to be in three to five years and what resources are required to get there? How much risk, particularly with your money, is it willing to take?

The best way to understand the borrower's environment is to ask management and then test the answers with your own experience and research. The answers you receive help form your view of management. Some of the best research comes from talking to the trade and competitors. You should focus on three areas:

1. *Market*. Ask why people buy your borrower's products and services? Does your borrower have a competitive advantage and is it sustainable?

2. *Industry*. Management should be able to describe trends in the industry and how the business is adapting to them. To put it in Darwinian terms, management must be able to tell you why the company will survive when others in the industry will not.

3. *Exogenous factors*. You should always understand how economic cycles affect your borrower. Management generally states that a recession will not affect the company for numerous reasons. After all, what management will tell a banker that a recession will kill the company? You should develop your own view. Also, determine if such factors as demographics, societal trends, or regulatory changes will have an effect.

The financial structure and results are ultimately a reflection of how management operates within its market environment. The financial goals of management are fairly straightforward, that is, maximize return on investment while remaining solvent. However, maximizing return and maintaining solvency can be in direct conflict. Management should have developed an operating philosophy concerning risk tolerance or how much return will be traded off to maintain solvency and flexibility.

Financial statement analysis is fundamentally a critical examination of liquidity, leverage, and cash flow in the past, present, and future to understand management's financial philosophy of return and solvency. Examination of the future, or projections, must examine how you think management will react to changes in the market, industry, and exogenous events. Your conclusions determine how you feel about the ultimate safety of your loan.

Unfortunately, many managements do not have well-articulated philosophies of return and solvency or risk tolerance. You might ask management how much it would leverage the company to meet return expectations. With higher leverage, the company has less room for error and fewer financing alternatives or flexibility. You may find that management has not really thought about risk and return, and you must coach these executives over time.

Part of the dilemma of management, particularly in smaller companies in which resources do not exist for functional specialization, is accomplishing all responsibilities with equal skill. For example, a farmer is basically engaged in production, marketing, and finance, yet few farmers seem equally adept in all three areas.

Your analysis of financial statements must be integrated with management's operations in its competitive environment as opposed to a recitation of arithmetic facts, which are already displayed in excruciating detail in the spreadsheets. If you cannot add value to what the computer has ground out, it is better to remain silent. This point will be illustrated in Chapter 5.

2. EXAMINING THE LOAN REQUEST

After examining the borrower, the second element of a loan decision is the loan request itself. At this point, you focus on purpose, payment, and protection (the second way out). The loan request is generally the most scrutinized in a credit write-up and is quite frequently the weakest. If this element is poorly developed, then structuring and monitoring will inevitably be weak as well. Clarity in this element creates a better credit decision and reflects favorably on the writer because clarity is, unfortunately, quite rare.

The purpose of a loan is fairly straightforward. On the books of the company, the journal entry is a debit to cash and a credit to notes payable when you make the loan. When the cash is expended, the reduction in cash is a credit, so the debit is the purpose of the loan. On the balance sheet, a debit increases assets, for example, inventories and fixed assets; decreases liabilities, for example, paying other debt; or decreases capital, for example, dividends, treasury stock, or expenses.

That's it. There are no other purposes of loan proceeds. When bankers say that the purpose of the loan is working capital, they have no idea where the money is going because they did not ask, they are poorly trained, or their managers tolerate sloppy practices.

A short-term note has no effect on working capital because it increases current assets and current liabilities equally. A loan could increase working capital if the loan were not repaid, if it were a permanent capital loan, or if it were a term loan. However, you still need to know the purpose because it may not increase current assets such as inventory. It may be used to buy fixed assets, repay other creditors' term debt, or alter capital through treasury stock purchases, dividends, or expenses.

I once encountered the following in a credit write-up: "The purpose of our loan is to provide a line of credit for working capital needs related to discretionary capital expenditures." Although this bit of blather had a certain humorous charm, I would have thought more of the writer if he had stated, "I have no idea where the money is going." Be clear on the purpose of your loan. If you do not know, ask the borrower to whom its checks will go.

Payment of the loan is less straightforward. If an increase in cash is a debit, what creates the cash is a credit. A credit reduces an asset, for example, collection of a receivable or sale of a fixed asset for cash; increases a liability, for example, refinancing; or increases capital, for example, new equity or retained earnings. Unfortunately, much of this happens simultaneously with offsetting factors such as cash being absorbed in increased current assets. You need projections on which you can perform sensitivity analysis to determine how wrong you can be.

Protection is determining if you have a second way out of your loan in case of failure of the primary source. A second way out of your loan is desirable because profit margins are so low in commercial lending that you cannot afford to take significant risk. The second way out usually involves collateral, guaranties, or another type of loan such as a term loan if there is any cash flow.

Inexperienced bankers invariably overestimate the value of collateral. You only need collateral when the borrower is defunct. Liquidation value has little relation to going-concern value, and you must know the difference. Ask yourself how you would get the books and records to collect directly from account debtors or how you would marshal the inventory and then sell it. Better yet, ask someone with liquidation experience.

3. STRUCTURING THE LOAN

Loan structuring can be defined as breaking down total debt into components in terms of repayment, that is, seasonal, term, bridge, and permanent capital and analyzing, documenting, pricing, and monitoring each component accordingly. Remember, cash is created to repay a loan from the conversion of a current asset, sale for cash of a noncurrent asset, refinancing, or increasing capital through new equity or retained earnings.

In terms of repayment, those four sources of cash can be grouped into three types of loans:

1. A seasonal loan, which is repaid from the conversion of current assets.
2. A term loan, which is repaid from an increase in retained earnings or cash generated from profitable operations.

3. A bridge loan, which is repaid from the sale of noncurrent assets, refinancing, or the infusion of equity.

In terms of repayment, there is a fourth type of loan and that is one for which you are not being repaid. You are, in effect, supplying permanent capital. Asset-based lending, floor planning, and feeder loans are examples of permanent capital lending in which monitoring the value of collateral is critical to the safety of your loan.

Therefore, there are only four types of loans in terms of repayment: seasonal, term, bridge, and permanent capital. There are no others. Note that the four types of loans have nothing to do with the purpose of the loan.

The trick of loan structuring is to isolate the borrower's financing requirement after considering the purposes of the loan and then break the financing requirement down into one or more of the four types of loans in terms of repayment. You can then analyze your repayment prospects for each type of loan, document and price them, and set your monitoring requirements.

Proper loan structuring is a powerful tool in managing a loan portfolio and demonstrates the degree of professionalism of the banker and manager. An old commercial lending adage states that a well-structured loan is half collected. Structuring ability is discussed in more detail later in this chapter.

4. MONITORING

Monitoring requirements flow naturally from the process of breaking the financing requirement down into one or more of the four types of loans in terms of repayment. With a seasonal loan, you focus more on the balance sheet and watch your peak debt position to ensure payout of your loan and the trade at the appropriate time. With a term loan, you emphasize the income statement and watch debt service and interest coverage.

You establish separate notes and facilities for each type of loan so that your seasonal loan is not funding payment on your term loan. Well-structured loans make a highly efficient portfolio. Each maturity means some action is to take place, so you have a built-in tickler system. Exceptions stand out and demand attention.

With a little imagination, you can obtain information from businesses that may not have the best interim financial data. For example, certain retail and service companies can easily supply you with monthly sales and trade payables numbers. You can estimate a break-even point and you know that if sales are declining and payables rising, you may have a problem. While no substitute for complete financial statements, tailor-made reporting can be useful and easily accomplished by your borrower.

If you design your monitoring list well, your exception reporting should reflect only potential problems as opposed to a long list of trivia that tends to bury the real issues. Exception reporting is a reflection of your artisanship, so a little time spent on carefully selected monitoring requirements ultimately reflects well on you.

5. Complying with Loan Policy

At some point in the loan decision process, you should pull back from the detail and ask yourself whether this loan makes sense in the context of what your bank is trying to accomplish in its commercial loan portfolio. This discipline is helpful in any decision where you are too close to the issues. Pulling back from the detail or "sleeping on it" can add a different perspective and clarity to your decision.

Discussing a potential loan with your manager and peers is the easiest way to determine loan policy compliance. Your manager should provide a forum in which loans can be discussed in a helpful and nonthreatening environment.

6. Weighing Risk versus Reward

In a commercial loan portfolio with a return on assets of 1.5-2.0%, there is little room for risk. You would not bet $100 at a racetrack in the hopes of winning $101.50. If your net charge-off ratio cannot exceed 0.5% on average, your loans must be close to a sure thing. Unfortunately, in overbanked markets, lenders rarely behave rationally. They tend to push down reward through lower pricing. Instead of reducing risk to equate to reduced reward, they increase risk through looser structure and moving down the credit scale.

The cyclical results of the banking industry over the past two decades illustrate this irrational behavior. Mitigating risk is the job of management and individual bankers. As a new banker, you must understand that the math of a bank's income statement is daunting.

One easy calculation illustrates this point. Multiply 0.5% by the outstandings of your department's commercial loan portfolio. The result should approximate the annual net charge-offs of the total portfolio. You can compare that result with budgeted charge-offs in your profit plan. Dividing the charge-off total by the number of lenders gives you a rough idea of your allocated share of charge-offs. Compare that number with your portfolio and with some of the larger credits in the portfolio. This sobering exercise demonstrates just how little room for error you have.

7. Establishing Loan Officer Commitment

Groups tend to make riskier decisions than individuals because a sense of accountability is lost in a group decision. Regardless of whether you have a committee or serial signature approval system, you must realize that you are responsible for the decision and every aspect of the loan until collection.

Even though responsibility for the decision can get fuzzy in a loan committee environment, you can be sure that it will be your loan if something goes wrong. Success has many fathers, while failure is a bastard.

Therefore, before you submit a loan to an approval process, ask yourself if you recommend it unhesitatingly and are fully committed to it. After all, you will own it.

To summarize the elements of a loan decision, you can expect the types of questions in the loan approval process that appear in Exhibit 4.1. Prepare yourself by asking your borrower similar questions or accomplishing the appropriate research.

LOAN STRUCTURE

Loan structuring demonstrates the art of commercial lending, for the banker, like an artisan, must tailor a solution that fits the needs of the borrower and the bank. Solutions can legitimately differ among bankers using different assumptions or with divergent views of the future. Because commercial bankers can never stop learning about structuring, the alert manager provides a forum for discussing cases in progress.

A logical and simple approach to loan structuring is to create a pro forma balance sheet that assumes the loan has been made. Take the most recent balance sheet and alter it in accordance with the purpose or purposes of the loan. You may add to inventories or fixed assets, or you may be change the debt or capital structure. Because the assets must equal the liabilities plus capital, the balancing or plug figure is the financing requirement.

Once the pro forma is completed, scan it to make sure it looks reasonable, paying particular attention to the position of other creditors. For example, if the business becomes highly leveraged, will the trade be as generous in terms as they were before the change in structure?

With the financing requirement established, you can now break it down into the four types of loans in terms of repayment and establish any subordinated debt or equity requirements. Note that you have already considered the purpose of the loan, which is irrelevant in the establishment of repayment. Break down the financing requirement in the following order:

EXHIBIT 4.1

LOAN DECISION QUESTIONS

I. **Analyzing the borrower**
   - A. Management
     1. Character—Do you want to do business with this company? Does management's life-style or personal payment habits raise any issues?
     2. Ability—What are management's strong and weak points? Can individuals recognize and adapt to change? How good is the contingency planning?
     3. Depth—What would happen in the absence of key managers?
     4. Vision—What will the company look like in three to five years?
   - B. Environment
     1. Why do people buy the company's products or services?
     2. Does it have a sustainable competitive advantage? What are the threats? Why will it be a survivor?
     3. What's happening in the industry?
     4. How will the company perform in a recession?
   - C. Financial statement analysis
     1. Historical financial data (past)
        - a. What do data mean in terms of liquidity, leverage, and cash flow?
        - b. How has the company financed itself?
        - c. What is management's philosophy concerning debt?
        - d. What relevance does history have to the future and repayment of our loan?
     2. Pro forma analysis (present)—What will the company look like if you make the loan?
     3. Projections (future)—How wrong can you be?

II. **Considering the loan request**
   - A Purpose—What is the company going to do with the money?
   - B. Payment—How is the company going to repay the loan?
   - C. Protection—What is your second way out? If you had to liquidate collateral, how would you do it, and what would you net?

III. **Structuring the loan**—What is the logic behind your selection of loan facilities?

IV. **Monitoring**
   - A. How are you going to follow the borrower until the loan is repaid?
   - B. Why did you select the covenants you are proposing?
   - C. How will the borrower assist you in the monitoring?

V. **Loan policy compliance**—Does this loan make sense given what the bank is trying to accomplish in its loan portfolio?

VI. **Risk/reward**—Is the bank getting paid enough for the risk it is taking?

VII. **Loan officer commitment**—Do you want to make this loan?

	Bridge loans
Commercial Lending	Seasonal loans
	Term loans
	Permanent capital loans
....	....
	Subordinated debt
Equity	Equity

BRIDGE LOANS

You start with bridge loans because they are so obvious and easy to spot. Bridge loans are repaid from the sale of noncurrent assets for cash, refinancing, or the infusion of equity, all of which are initiated by management decisions.

If a building is to be sold within 60 days and you are confident that it will happen because there is a purchase contract with a deposit, you could establish a 60-day note for the amount of the proceeds and deduct that amount from the financing requirement. Lending is rarely that easy. You are usually confronted with management's desire to sell an asset, the hope that a long-term lender will be interested, or the possibility of an uncle putting in some equity.

The trick is deciding how likely the sale, refinancing, or equity infusion will be and what happens if there is a failure or delay.

SEASONAL LOANS

After examining the financing requirement for a bridge loan opportunity, look for the possibility of a seasonal loan. Obtain monthly or quarterly balance sheets and look for the seasonal expansion and contraction of current assets. If the borrower is a customer, you also can examine your borrowing history and note high and low outstandings and any cleanups.

Borrowers with seasonal components are usually fairly obvious, for example, toy manufacturers and plant nurseries. You must project their peak borrowing time and needs and decide how comfortable you are with the inventory and receivables that will ultimately repay you.

Ensure that the amount of your seasonal facility is small enough to permit a real cleanup without leaning on the trade. The cleanup is extremely important when you have other types of loan facilities. For example, if you have a term loan and there is no cleanup of your seasonal facility, you are probably advancing on your seasonal facility to make term loan payments.

If there is a seasonal component, isolate it through your analysis of peaks and valleys in current assets and supporting debt, and then subtract it from your financing requirement.

TERM LOANS

Term loans demand an extensive analysis of projected cash flows and an understanding of the borrower's market and position in the industry. Cash generated from profitable operations has masters other than your term loan to serve. In fact, you are one of several competitors for available cash flow.

If the company is growing, it must maintain some reasonable relationship between sales and working capital. If this relationship is strained, the company will be "over-trading" and probably constantly scrambling for cash. Cash flow can be absorbed to maintain the balance between sales and working capital. Cash flow also can be used for noncurrent asset acquisitions, payments on existing term debt, and dividend payments or treasury stock purchases. What is left over is available to service your new term debt.

How much of a term loan you are willing to extend is, therefore, a function of how much cash flow is available to service it, what secondary sources of repayment are available, and how long a loan you are willing to make, which is a loan policy issue. Once you have isolated the amount of the term loan, subtract it from the remainder of the financing requirement.

PERMANENT CAPITAL LOANS

If there is any financing requirement left at this point, examine the liquidation value of the assets to determine the potential of making a permanent capital or asset-based loan. If your bank does not specialize in asset-based lending but you are willing to make such a loan in the case under question, be sure you are satisfied with the long-term viability of the borrower.Leave plenty of margin, so your loan will be attractive to an asset-based lending specialist in case of deterioration.

Asset-based lending is not for the fainthearted, and your bank's management should have a clear policy on how far it is willing to go in this field and when the loan should be handed off to a professional. The policy should set forth minimum administrative standards, margin guidelines, audit procedures, and so forth.

With bridge, seasonal, term, and well-secured and administered permanent capital loans, you are operating in the realm of commercial banking with 1.5-2.0% return on assets and average tolerances for net charge-offs in the 0.25-0.75% range. Because pricing leaves little margin for error in an overbanked environment, lenders need well-defined purposes, logical structure, and second ways out.

Few borrowing situations have all four types of loans, but two is certainly common. Even with existing customers, you should periodically analyze the financial requirement to see if your original assumptions are still valid. You may find that because of rapid growth or other reasons, your seasonal or term loan should now be more properly structured as a permanent capital loan.

What happens if you add up the bridge, seasonal, term, and permanent capital potential loans and you still have some financing requirement left over? Then you are in the equity realm and must behave differently.

EQUITY

In the equity realm, you are quite low in the food chain of claimants against the borrower's resources. Banks operate in the equity realm for four reasons:

1. *Overadvances*. You may suddenly find that you are overadvanced on the collateral you are monitoring in a permanent capital loan or the repayment on a bridge loan was less than anticipated. To your credit, your monitoring procedures are good, so you know immediately that you have a problem. After discussing the situation with your manager, you meet with the borrower and establish a separate note for the overadvance, reprice it, negotiate a repayment program, and ask for additional collateral or guaranties. Spotting, reacting, and curing overadvances are all part of a day's work for good commercial lenders.
2. *Temporary overadvances*. While structuring the financing requirement, you conclude that the total of the four types of loans is slightly short of the requirement. Instead of stretching collateral values, you are honest about identifying the shortfall. Your bank should have a policy about how to handle temporary overadvances, including analysis, amount, term, pricing, and so forth. Your bank's policy might permit you to isolate the overadvance on a separate, higher priced note, amortizing monthly over 12 months subject to intense analysis and higher internal approvals.
3. *Policy*. Some banks, by policy, have established separate, highly disciplined units that make subordinated loans and equity investments. Understanding the true nature of the risk, these units attempt to yield roughly twice that of a commercial lender on subordinated or mezzanine loans and three times on equity investments. If you are making a loan above subordinated debt, read the agreements to understand how deeply subordinated the debt really is.
4. *Cluelessness*. Unfortunately, a distressingly large number of banks operate unwittingly in the equity section at commercial loan pricing with no idea of the risks involved. This incredibly sloppy lending practice results from lack of training in structure and inadequate policies. This type of lending is characterized by constantly rolling over debt with no real idea of purpose

or payment. If this type of malpractice is prevalent in a market, borrowers believe that banks are sources of capital rather than loans with defined purposes and repayment schedules. An understanding of the four types of loans and their role in loan structuring enables you to explain to a borrower where commercial lending ends and equity begins. If you are not a provider of equity, and most banks are not, then you can explain to your borrower's management that raising equity is its responsibility.

OBJECTIONS

In the sale of products and services, the customer is likely to raise specific objections that should be anticipated. A good sales manager holds periodic objection training sessions at which objections on new and existing products are discussed and role playing helps lenders respond to the objections.

In the field of lending, borrowers raise common objections as well as market-specific objections. Because the competitive market is in a constant state of flux, objections should be periodically reviewed, particularly in markets with illogical or erratic competitors. It is much easier to compete with professionals.

The first step in dealing with objections is to listen to the customer. Listening is not a passive art. Good listening is more difficult than speaking. You decipher what the customer is saying, what he or she is not saying, and what he or she wants to say. Good listening skills require training and self-appraisal.

The following objections are fairly common in lending but have market-specific permutations. Your manager should include these in sales training but relies on you for feedback on new objections you encounter in the marketplace.

PRICING

The commercial lending markets are not particularly efficient, so you will encounter significant pricing differentials. It may pay to subscribe to a pricing service that follows pricing nationally and regionally. You can try to point out to your customer that your bank attempts to be fully competitive in pricing, if not a leader, and that no institution can remain uncompetitive for long. At any time in an inefficient market, there will be price differences, but these differences tend to equalize over time. A borrower should beware of the bank that pitches the low introductory offer and then raises rates in the future. Chasing rate differentials is not a particularly efficient use of time and destroys the value added by professional relationship management.

Always calculate the net after-tax value of, say, 0.25% or 0.50% using the customer's interest expense from historical statements. If the borrower is not leveraged, you may find that the net after-tax effect of what is in dispute is actually negligible to the customer. To a leveraged institution like a bank whose business is deposit intermediation, 0.25% is significant. It may mean little to the customer.

If you have a close relationship with the customer and you have been responsive and have added value, do not hesitate to point out that your bank's professionalism is worth some interest rate differential. You must know your customer to push this point, but you may be surprised to find that pricing is not the number one issue.

Personal Guaranty

If your borrower is owned or controlled by management, a personal guaranty is a logical requirement of lending. After all, management can do whatever it wants with the company's assets. Also, the bank frequently has more at risk in the company than the owner's net worth. If the company develops problems, you want the full cooperation and commitment of management.

You never know true character until it is tested, and through the psychological process of denial, borrowers often transfer the cause of failure to their banks. Nothing is more frustrating than being tossed the keys by an owner who promises to help you collect the receivables for a consulting fee. It happens. Ask anyone in workout about the value of personal guaranties.

Unfortunately, many banks give up personal guaranties as a competitive weapon in their search for volume. Unprofessional behavior feels good in the short run but is painful long term. It also ruins a marketplace.

If your borrower objects to a personal guaranty, find out why. It is somewhat illogical for a borrower to claim the company can repay the loan yet not be confident enough to commit personal assets.

You may be able to find acceptable compromises. If the owner has little outside of the borrowing company, a limited guaranty may preserve commitment and be effectively as good as an unlimited guaranty while being palatable to the guarantor. You might consider excluding specific assets that are important to the customer but have no value to you.

You also might explain to your borrower under what conditions, if any, you would release a guaranty. These conditions are usually covered in the loan policy and should be discussed with your manager. However, in particular circumstances, you might consider foregoing a guaranty if the borrower achieves a certain debt/equity ratio or debt-service coverage.

COLLATERAL

An owner who personally guarantees his or her company should insist that you take collateral. After all, the guarantor would rather you be paid than other creditors. I once had a guarantor audit my security interest filings.

Should the owner object to collateral, find out why. If the objection has something to do with obtaining trade credit, you may be able to work out an acceptable compromise.

COVENANTS

Covenants should not be considered controls; they are really a common understanding and belief about the future direction of the borrower and your relationship. Covenants are normally based on information and projections furnished by the borrower. If the borrower objects to a covenant, ask what is behind the concern. You then may be able to rewrite the covenant to mutual satisfaction.

Without giving up any rights, you should state that a covenant violation would indicate a serious change in direction from the mutually developed view of the direction of the company. You would want to meet with management immediately, determine the issues, and work out a mutually acceptable course of action. A covenant violation rarely means an immediate attempt to collect the loan.

SALARY LIMITATIONS

Although perfectly understandable from a lender's point of view, salary limitations can raise serious ego issues. You might be able to achieve the same result by designing a minimum debt-service or earnings covenant. Again, the negotiating trick is to discover the real concern of the borrower and find an acceptable solution.

SUMMARY

The loan request rarely comes nicely packaged. You must develop information from interviews and research and then determine if the request meets your loan policy. If it does not, then you must attempt to negotiate a mutually acceptable proposal that you can submit to your loan approval process.

As you develop the request, ensure that it fits into the sequential process of loan administration in your organization. Loan administration is a logical progression of events that can be broken down into five steps: loan policy, loan approval, monitoring, loan review, and problem loan administration.

Chapter 5

Loan Approval

Once the loan request has been examined, structured, and reviewed with the borrower, you must obtain internal approval before a commitment can be extended. This stage requires delicacy and caution because you must negotiate enough detail to form a tangible proposal without committing the bank before approval.

At the same time, you must represent the bank and not defer to some distant authority such as a credit committee. If you refer responsibility to a committee, your customer will rightly conclude that it is a waste of time to deal with you and ask to be introduced to the committee.

Obtaining internal approval usually consists of two phases, the credit write-up and the approval process. The write-up is an integral part of approval and also serves as a permanent record of the transaction and its logic. The loan approval process tests the transaction against loan policy using what is hoped to be the accumulated wisdom of the institution.

The credit write-up and the loan approval process are at the very heart of the organization's credit function. In fact, there are few other occasions in which your talents and abilities are so exposed. Obviously, mastery of these two phases is essential to your and your bank's success.

THE CREDIT WRITE-UP

No document in banking is as universally criticized as the credit write-up. Most experienced credit personnel readily admit it is an overly lengthy piece of tedium that misses the salient issues while regurgitating data that are available elsewhere. Novice lenders look on the write-up as a college exam dumping in all retained knowledge in the hopes that the correct answer lies somewhere within. This bilge is then perpetuated in word-processing programs in which irrelevant numbers are updated annually.

That so few credit people have successfully changed this practice is an acknowledgment of hidebound conservatism or the inability to accomplish beneficial change in a bureaucracy. Many have tried to improve write-ups by limiting available space or demanding the use of bullet points. Most have been borne from the arena on their shields.

The tragedy is not just the tremendous cost of processing useless paper, assuming that if it is written, someone must read it. More important, your writing is a reflection of your thought process and fully exposes your logic and critical thinking abilities. The well-written, succinct document that extracts the essential from complexity is such a rare event that the stature of such a writer is elevated immediately in the eyes of readers.

In fairness, the credit write-up attempts to accomplish many different ends for a wide audience. The banker may consider it the repository of basic information, while the credit committee just wants the facts on a specific transaction. The manager may be afraid of criticism from loan review so asks for everything to be on the safe side. The loan reviewer grumbles about plowing through irrelevant data just to determine if the fundamental risks are addressed. The input function wants basic facts, such as amount, rate, maturity, commitment type. Examiners want an understanding of the risk and how the loan relates to the credit process.

Because of the timing of the receipt of annual financial information, many banks have a credit write-up season, generally in April and May. Productive activity virtually stops as bankers grind out renewals under intense deadline pressure. Creative thinking is overwhelmed.

There is no reason why the workload cannot be distributed evenly throughout the year. Some seasonal credits are not logically timed for their fiscal statements. Many borrowers have perfectly good internal reporting with minimal year-end adjustments. These credits can be redistributed with the audits confirming internal reporting.

Good writing skills are difficult to teach. They require immediate feedback, one-on-one coaching, and rewriting. In the meantime, a customer is waiting. Many managers find it is easier to obtain the answers orally and hope that the next write-up will be better. It rarely is.

The best way to improve your writing skills is to obtain objective feedback. Ask your manager for an honest assessment of the quality of your credit write-ups, and if deficiencies are noted, schedule a time when you can review some examples together. Use completed transactions, so you do not have the time pressure of responding immediately to a customer.

If your manager is unavailable or unhelpful, search out a mentor. Perhaps someone in loan review or the credit function would be delighted to coach you. After all, they read many write-ups.

The following discussion is offered to give you some insight into making your credit write-ups stand out. It is no substitute for honest feedback and active coaching and counseling. Also, no amount of writing skill can cover up lazy thinking. Your writing reflects your critical thinking skills.

PURPOSE

The purpose of the write-up should be to justify the credit extensions contained therein. Every sentence should focus on this mission and add value to it. Naturally, the credit file has much more data, including competitive information, résumés of management, industry analyses, and trade reports. Use common sense. New credits should contain more background information than older customers that are well known to management.

The credit write-up is not a sales tool. Be objective and candid about strengths and weaknesses and potential risks to the bank. Remember that most people reading credit write-ups have had years of experience in both writing and reacting to these documents. They can easily recognize a snow job.

What readers want is fairly simple. See Exhibit 5.1 for a brief summary.

The document should contain your opinions and conclusions of analysis and reflect your judgment. For example, most readers do not want to plow

EXHIBIT 5.1

CREDIT WRITE-UP

Given this information concerning management, the company, and its position in the market and industry, all of which is relevant to the credit decision, the customer has requested funds for the following specific needs....

We propose to fund these needs and will structure the following types of loan facilities in terms of repayment....

The primary source of repayment for each facility is....and is reliable because....

The secondary sources of repayment are .... They are reliable/weak because....

The main risks to repayment are....

We have mitigated these risks by....

Our strategy for administering the credit is....

through legal opinions and collateral audits. They would rather have you state, "We have a perfected security interest in the collateral and the liquidation value is adequate to cover our loan." Being forthright requires a little courage. However, if you recommend the loan and are committed to it, you should have already arrived at such conclusions and should not be afraid to state them.

THEME OF THE CREDIT

Most borrowing customers have a dominant theme that is relevant to your extension of credit. Before you start writing, think about the nature of this theme. If you are new to the credit, it may take time and numerous discussions with management to understand the issue.

Themes are not just financial, although many are. They may be related to management, the competitive market, and the industry. Some examples of themes relevant to credit extensions are:

- *Undercapitalization*. A leveraged company should have strong, predictable cash flows and operate in a relatively stable market and industry. If these requirements are not met, the long-term viability of the borrower is questionable.
- *Management*. Management may be perfectly competent at a given company size, especially when the owner is a hands-on entrepreneur. If the company is growing, at what point should the owner add professional management in the form of a chief financial officer, sales manager, or production manager? Will the owner be willing to do so?
- *Succession*. Many management-owned companies generate enough cash flow to support the owner adequately. Is there enough earning power to support the owner plus sons and daughters and their families?
- *Markets*. Does the business have a sustainable competitive advantage? For example, how will a main street retailer compete with a suburban discounter?
- *Industry*. Industry changes are generally subtle with new characteristics evolving over time. Is the outlook for the family practice clinic on which you have a term loan the same today as it was five years ago?

Themes of credit can be challenges or opportunities for the business involved. If you can recognize them successfully, they can help you structure your loans. For example, if your borrower's sustainable competitive advantage is unclear, you should be less willing to extend term credit. Recognizing the theme of a credit also helps you focus your efforts in the credit write-up.

THE TRANSACTION

Although describing the proposed credit facilities in the credit write-up sounds relatively straightforward, an unusual amount of time is often spent in the approval process trying to understand the deal. Readers generally want to know purpose, payment, and protection or, put another way, where the money is going, what the loan structure is in terms of repayment, and what collateral is offered.

Perhaps part of the problem is caused by standardized formats that are used as input documents. It is very difficult to design standard documents for highly customized transactions. When faced with a customizing situation, fill in the form so the input is correct but add an explanatory note such as Exhibit 5.2.

There are numerous variations to the approach in Exhibit 5.2. You could start with a summary balance sheet before the loan is made, illustrate sources and uses of funds, and then provide a pro forma. You could go into more detail on administration of the permanent capital loan if it is not done elsewhere. You could discuss cash flow adequacy for the term loan at this point.

Although there can and should be many variations of style, the point is to illustrate clearly the purpose of the loan, your structuring, and the second way out. Subsequent sections of your write-up in which you discuss management, the business, financial analysis, and strategy should then reinforce the logic of your loan structuring.

MANAGEMENT

Although the assessment of management is absolutely critical to a loan decision, you can be quite brief on this subject in a credit write-up. Critical analysis of strengths and weaknesses are probably best reserved for oral commentary in the approval process.

There are, however, two areas that deserve comments: management's plans or direction for the business and management's financial philosophy. If these are not well articulated, you should attempt to develop them over time in consultative discussions with management. Owners of small businesses are so absorbed in daily operations that many have given little thought to such broader issues as direction and financial philosophy. If that is the case in a particular credit, say so in your write-up and move on to the next section.

Any comments you do make on management should assist in the assessment of the transaction you described previously. If they do not, they are probably superfluous. Because management is such an integral part of a credit decision, commentary on management will be intertwined with discussions of the business, financial analysis, and strategy.

EXHIBIT 5.2

EXPLANATORY NOTE TO STANDARDIZED TRANSACTION FORM

Wakefield Manufacturing Company has been a customer for 30 years. We financed the company at inception, but its profitability has been so strong and predictable that we have been totally paid out for about 10 years. We have extended a $2 million line for window dressing. It has never been used.

John Wakefield, who has not been active in the company for three years, has asked the company to purchase his 50% interest. Frank and Paul Renville, the remaining shareholders at 25% each, have agreed on a purchase price of $5 million, of which we will lend $4 million and Wakefield will carry back a deeply subordinated note of $1 million. Upon completion of the transaction, the pro forma balance sheet will look like this:

(000s omitted)			
Cash	$ 125	Payables & accruals	$ 2,100
Receivables	1,950	Bank outstandings	4,000
Inventory	2,475	Subordinated debt	1,000
Fixed assets	5,450	Equity	2,900
	$10,000		$10,000

Our $4 million in outstandings at closing is structured as follows:

- $500,000 bridge loan maturing in 60 days secured by former warehouse space in the process of being sold. There is a purchase contract with a $50,000 deposit in place. In the unlikely event that the property cannot be sold, there is $1 million in unused availability under the permanent capital facility.
- $2.5 million term loan payable in equal monthly installments over seven years. This loan is secured by a first mortgage on plant, office, and warehouse space with an appraised value of $3.75 million for a loan-to-value ratio of 67%. Historical cash flow is adequate to service this debt (see financial analysis). Payment on subordinated debt is not allowed until our term loan is repaid.
- $1 million permanent capital loan. This is the initial advance under a $2 million facility. Collateral eligibility would permit the total facility to be drawn down.

When considering management's plans or direction for the business, try to isolate factors that could affect your credit. For example, if you are proposing a term loan, the following examples might be relevant:

- Robert Jenkins is the leader of an investment group that purchased this company from near bankruptcy two years ago. Through rigorous restructuring and expense controls, the group has turned the company around, and it is showing modest profits. Now the group is aggressively entering new markets to demonstrate an increasing trend in revenues and earnings with the intent of selling the company in three to five years at a significant profit. The group will leverage the company and do what it takes to achieve this goal.

- William Parkerson professes no desire to expand his business beyond the somewhat protected and profitable niche in which he operates. With the strong cash flows and positive outlook for the company, he wants to provide a retirement fund for himself and, in approximately 10 years, turn a profitable and conservatively capitalized company over to his son.

Financial philosophies are frequently well articulated in larger companies that must be responsive to a shareholding public. For example, a company might state that it desires to maintain a BBB+ to AA debt rating, an 18-20% return on equity, and compound earnings and dividend growth of 8-12%. In smaller management-owned companies, you may need to do a little gentle prodding over time to achieve a similar statement. Again, the issue is how management's philosophy might affect your credit. Consider the following example:

> As the sole owner, Gary Thompson considers successful performance of the business in terms of his salary, additions to his tax-deferred retirement account, and growth in personal and business net worth. He would like to draw $100,000 to $125,000 in salary and add 5-7% of pretax profits to his retirement accounts. His view of the balance sheet is less developed. He likes to retire equipment debt in three years, so he will always be in a position to buy new machinery. He is comfortable with current leverage and sees no need to increase it.

Ideally, management will develop a financial philosophy relating to performance expectations of the company and how much risk it is willing to take to achieve them. Tangible expressions of this philosophy can be made in debt ratings, leverage ratios, debt-service coverage, return on equity, and earnings and dividend or draw growth rates. If you and management can develop a financial philosophy, you will have a much better understanding of the risk in your credit.

THE BUSINESS

If the readers are unfamiliar with the business, a brief description of its activities is appropriate. Readers do not want exhaustive narrations on every product and market niche, particularly when it is copied from annual reports and other company literature. Remember that whatever you say should aid understanding of the credit risk described in your transaction section. It is impossible to separate management from the business, so comments on this relationship are also appropriate.

In discussing the business, there are three areas in which you may choose to focus. First, determine if the business has a sustainable competitive advantage in its marketplace. Second, describe changes in the industry and how they might affect your credit. Third, examine exogenous events such as business cycles, interest rates, commodity prices, and demographic changes to determine how they will affect your borrower and your credit risk. These areas of focus and comments on management can all be included in one brief statement such as:

- Building Materials Inc. manufactures concrete blocks for the construction trade in Madison and Laketon counties. The large investment in fixed assets and high transportation costs have sheltered the company from intense competition in this market niche. Earnings are influenced by building cycles and energy costs. Nevertheless, the company has remained marginally profitable in periods of low construction activity and high fuel prices. Continued growth in construction activity produces solid profitability in the short run but may attract competitors that are reportedly studying this market. Long-term profitability should continue to be volatile, and management agrees that capital investment and the debt to finance it should have a short payback of about three years.
- Jacob Bolton has been in the auto parts manufacturing business for 25 years and has experienced business cycles, foreign competition, changes in vendor relations, just-in-time inventories, and the total quality movement. His management team is very adaptable to a changing environment, and the company has sustained only two minor loss years during this period. Our seasonal loans are based on contracts in hand, and equipment financing has been modest and repaid over three years. Capacity could become tight, and management shares our concerns about future capital investment in the face of erratic earnings. Although nothing is being considered currently, continued outsourcing in the industry could produce a need for significantly expanded capacity.
- Susan Walden's company has been in business for three years supplying components to personal computer manufacturers. Growth has been exceptional, but the customer list is narrowly concentrated. Production is fairly labor-intensive, and barriers to entry do not appear significant. Trade and competitor checks indicate that this work could easily be done by com-

puter manufacturers, but as long as the price is right, the manufacturers prefer to use manufacturing space for higher value input and have fewer people to manage. The company has never experienced a downturn, and management is untested in adversity. Our permanent capital loan is based on receivables with a low inventory cap. Management is constantly requesting funds for fixed-asset expansion, which we feel should be provided by equity. If we cannot arrange term financing or if the company can find a more liberal lender, we may very well lose a good asset-based loan.

Your comments on the business will necessarily involve discussions on management and should always bear in mind the effect on your credit risk. Readers are looking for your analysis and opinion, so you should not be afraid of being judgmental and subjective.

FINANCIAL ANALYSIS

When discussing historical data, ask yourself if your analysis furthers an understanding of the transactions you have described and reflects your views of management and the business. Focus on how the company has financed itself and the use of your debt. Do not repeat information that an experienced reader can gather directly from the financial spreadsheets. Write explanations directly on the spreadsheets using asterisks or footnotes. For example, intangibles, loans to or from insiders, other bank debt, subordinated debt, and so forth demand detail that can be handwritten on the spreads.

Consider the following analysis:

> For the three years under consideration, sales increased 12% and 18% with a compound growth rate of 14.9%. Gross profit dropped from 25.3% to 24.1% to 23.9%. Although profit before taxes increased from $1.3 million to $1.344 million to $1.388 million, profit as a percentage of sales fell from 5.4% to 4.8% to 4.2%. Sales/working capital went from 6.9x to 10.2x to 13.1x. Days receivables deteriorated from 38 days to 46 days to 55 days, while inventory slowed from 43 days to 59 days to 68 days. Payable days went from 45 days to 41 days to 35 days. Sales to net fixed assets increased from 5x to 8x to 12x. Debt to worth increased from 1.4 to 2.8 to 3.9.

Obviously, something quite significant is happening to this company, but this analysis does little to disclose what it is. The writer has prepared the classical elevator analysis (leverage went up, payable days went down), which the reader could obtain more efficiently by going directly to the spreads. A more useful approach might be:

> Gene Stapleton considers sales volume to be virtually the only measurement of success and the bigger the increase, the better. He is content if profits rise from one year to the next and has no concept of cash flow generation versus earnings. To increase sales growth, Stapleton is expanding beyond his traditional, protected market niche and is establishing vendor relationships with large discounters in the region. Predictably, his gross profits are dropping, and selling expenses are rising as he has added two salespeople to tackle this new market. Consequently, profitability is anemic, although Stapleton will argue that it is rising.
>
> The discounters are stretching receivables and demanding faster delivery times, so more inventory must be kept on hand. A check with suppliers indicates that the trade is becoming a little nervous because of increasing leverage and is no longer willing to extend generous terms. Stapleton is overtrading working capital, and our seasonal loan has become a permanent capital loan. Warehouse space is being stretched, and although Stapleton would like to add capacity, we have told him he is not generating sufficient cash to finance additional fixed assets.

Although this analysis contains no numbers, it gives the reader a much better understanding of the issues. It also involves the loan transaction, management, and the approach of the business to its market. Try to write a financial analysis without numbers. It forces you to think of the factors producing the results rather then to just describe the results.

Your discussion of projections should focus on the margin of error for your loan. For example, on a seasonal loan, you might examine your position in relation to that of the trade when the greatest risk occurs, often at the time of peak inventory. What could prevent the conversion of inventory to receivables to cash?

On a term loan, you might illustrate your most likely cash projections and then examine the key drivers of cash flow such as sales growth, gross margin, selling, general, and administrative expenses, asset and liability turns, and capital expenditures. Through sensitivity analysis, you can isolate two or three drivers that have the most impact on cash generation and discuss how wrong you could be and still have a viable loan.

The financial analysis gives you an opportunity to stand out because a good analysis will relate the credit to the results produced by management in its market and industry. This analysis then logically leads to the strategy for the administration of the credit.

STRATEGY

The strategy should be a brief description of how you will administer the credit given your conclusions concerning the transaction, management, business, and financial analysis. If the previous sections are well written, the strategy should be fairly obvious. For example, the following might be your strategy for the Gene Stapleton credit just analyzed:

> The growth rate of Stapleton's business may begin to decelerate because he has somewhat saturated his market, and transportation expenses will begin to restrict additional sales. Because of his penchant for growth, moderation is in no means certain, as he may take on new lines or territories. Our asset-based loan is currently well protected as receivable quality is excellent and inventory is not subject to obsolescence. Discounters may push inventory back to the company, but I feel it can be resold. I have discussed the eligibility requirements with our asset-based lending unit to confirm that they are conservative. We advance on borrowing certificates, apply receivables proceeds to the loan, and audit collateral semiannually. Stapleton understands that if there is a covenant violation, the loan will be immediately transferred to asset-based lending. He is not completely comfortable with this arrangement and, if it happens, would probably attempt to refinance with a more liberal lender.

Although every bank has its own format for credit write-ups, a logical discussion of the transaction, management, business, financial analysis, and strategy can generally be included. This approach disciplines you to focus on elements affecting the credit and gives the reader an understanding of the risk and your skill as a responsible lender. The write-up then becomes the vehicle for loan approval.

THE APPROVAL PROCESS

The credit approval process in most banks is generally a credit committee or a serial signature system or some hybrid of the two. One common theme that unites all approval processes is the lack of periodic evaluation of effectiveness. Although this is a management problem, you must learn to deal with whatever is in place. The alert manager periodically seeks comments and suggestions from the people who must deal with the process.

Whichever process your bank uses, the purpose is still to test individual transactions against the loan policy and approve, modify, or reject them. Each system has advantages and disadvantages and can potentially accomplish much more than merely approving a transaction.

THE CREDIT COMMITTEE

The credit committee is probably the predominant system of credit approval in the industry, although the rapidly changing environment is causing some reevaluation. At its best, the credit committee offers the following:

- *Expertise*. The committee can bring to bear on a single transaction some of the best credit minds in the organization. Individuals on the committee may have long memories and unique experiences that can be powerful competitive tools.
- *Training*. A good committee environment also provides a learning experience and offers continuous training for all lenders.
- *Communications*. The committee can provide a forum for communicating information about the customers making up the loan portfolio.
- *Culture*. If the credit culture is weak, the committee can be a bully pulpit for instituting change.

However, at its worst, the credit committee has some significant faults:

- *Dominance*. The committee can be dominated by one person, in which case the experience and wisdom of others is not used and their time is wasted.
- *Risk*. Unless individual responsibility is constantly reinforced, committees tend to make riskier decisions because accountability is lost.
- *Efficiency*. Rigid meeting schedules tend to slow down responsiveness and take bankers out of action for extended periods. Depending on the size of the committee, massive amounts of paper must be processed. Some committee members, often outside directors, add little credit knowledge and could be better used in policy formation.
- *Preparation*. Ideally, every committee member reads the credit write-ups in advance and notes points needing clarification. This preparation speeds up the process and prevents frustrating the person who has prepared a good write-up. If appropriate homework has not been accomplished, it becomes quite apparent at the meeting and generates resentment. Members should compliment the writers of good documents but can only do so if they have read them.
- *Exhaustion*. By the end of lengthy and tedious sessions, most members are brain-dead. Consequently, attention is applied unevenly. Easier credits at the beginning of the meeting may receive too much attention, and riskier deals at the end may receive too little.

- *Limits*. Lending limits are often too low or risk is not considered in the process. Expertise is, therefore, applied unevenly to the problems.

Most credit committees operate somewhere between these extremes but provide ample opportunity for improvement. At least annually, the manager should solicit comments about the process and determine how much time is being expended. This analysis should determine if the institution is receiving full value for the considerable efforts expended.

SERIAL SIGNATURES

The serial signature system, too, has advantages and disadvantages. It can be quite effective when it is difficult to meet as a committee because of travel schedules or locations. With unusual transactions, signers can meet with the lender and benefit from the advantages of a committee without its rigidity.

If the serial signature system loses its flexibility, it has many disadvantages. The unfortunate lender may end up telling the same story several different times to different people in the hierarchy. If there are more than approximately four signers on the approval document, it is doubtful that succeeding signers are adding value, but they are certainly slowing down responsiveness. Often signers assume, perhaps incorrectly, that the last signer has really scrutinized the transaction, so they need not bother.

ADAPTATION

Although you can hope that your manager will solicit suggestions for keeping the approval process relevant, you must work with what you have. The following are a few suggestions for dealing with a loan approval process:

- Always prepare a good credit write-up, as you will be judged by its quality. If someone has obviously not read the document and asks you a question that you have clearly answered, politely refer to the correct page and then give an oral response.
- Make note of the questions being asked, as they generally express valid concerns. Ask yourself if they should have been covered in your write-up or if they are clarifications or amplifications of points you have raised.
- Do not force an issue. Your ego is not at stake. Remember, you are an advocate for both the customer and the shareholder in a process designed to test the transaction against loan policy. It is not a sales process in which you push the good and gloss over the bad. If there is conflict, it is usually caused by a lack of clarity in loan policy.
- Devote as much effort to listening as speaking and vow to learn something from each presentation. If you were wrong, learn from it.

- On particularly difficult or new transactions, prepare members or signers in advance. You and your manager might brief the appropriate approver before soliciting a new credit customer to obtain a "fishing license." Or you might take the approver on a call to gather firsthand experience.

SUMMARY

Few documents in banking expose your skills, judgment, and understanding as much as the credit write-up. Develop the theme of the credit and then integrate the transaction into a discussion of management, the business, and financial analysis leading to a logical strategy for administering the loan and dealing with the customer.

Although the credit write-up is the vehicle for the loan approval process, your presentation skills will be tested in the discussion of the transaction. As an advocate of both the customer and the shareholder, you must maintain an appropriate balance of loyalties.

Chapter 6

The Loan Closing

When you develop a loan request with your customer, you walk a fine line by shaping the transaction in enough substance to present for internal approval without making a commitment until that approval is received. With approval in hand, you can now negotiate the final details including specific covenants, so the loan can proceed to closing.

The loan approval process normally approves a general framework for the credit, allowing you some room to maneuver when negotiating the details. This procedure raises the issue of when you must go back to loan approval if the negotiated details are different than the ones that were approved. Obviously, only material changes that have a real impact on risk should be resubmitted.

Changes that are material are a matter of judgment but also can be a barometer of the state of the credit culture. If insignificant changes are being resubmitted to credit approval, lenders may be insecure, excessively afraid of criticism, or unwilling to take responsibility for their decisions.

As a new lender, you probably have little idea of what is material to a distant credit committee. Until you learn the ropes, ask your manager. Do not fall into the habit of resubmitting trivia just to cover your backside.

After receiving internal approval, you will go through the process of negotiating final details, such as specific covenants, preparing documents, dealing with lawyers if involved, closing, and then monitoring the borrower. Mastery of each step makes you highly productive and well received by your customers, and it ensures that the job is much more enjoyable.

COVENANTS

After receiving internal approval, you negotiate the final form of the transaction with your customer. Unless you have a very short-term loan, this negotiation involves setting covenants. Covenants require monitoring, which is an expensive and time-consuming process. Consequently, they must be efficiently designed and kept to a minimum.

PURPOSE

Covenants communicate a common understanding and set of expectations for both borrower and lender. If the covenants are met, the borrower is entitled to the peace of mind of knowing that funding will continue under the terms outlined. If the covenants are not met, the bank, after the agreed grace period, can stop funding and reconsider its position.

Covenants are derived from management's projections of how the company will perform. Consequently, management should feel confident in them. In fact, management generally uses the adjective conservative to describes the projections given bankers. If management objects strenuously to covenants based on its own projections, find out why.

Covenant violations should signal a fundamental change in risk in the company before it is no longer attractive to other financial institutions. The ideal financial covenant might be set to correspond with a change in risk rating. For example, the major rating agencies have used debt-service ratios and leverage as major components in establishing their ratings for more than a century. You should find out if there is a significant correlation between these two ratios and your own risk-rating designations. A study of this correlation might give you some useful guidelines for setting covenants.

Covenants are important to loan portfolio management. In a bond portfolio, the rating on an individual bond may be downgraded with no event of default occurring. However, there is an efficient market for the bond even if sold at a loss. If the risk changes on a significant number of commercial loans, the overall risk of the portfolio is affected. Bank management needs the ability to disengage from such borrowers as it would have in a bond portfolio, or it should be able to restructure the transactions with pricing and collateral that reflect the new risks.

SELECTION

The list of available financial and nonfinancial covenants is massive. The art of covenant selection is designing the minimum requirements to keep your risk the same as when the loan was made while preserving cash within the borrowing company.

One approach to selecting financial covenants is to first ensure that you receive adequate and timely financial reporting at an appropriate frequency. Then, limit yourself to two or three financial covenants per type of loan in terms of repayment. Many covenants will overlap and will not be repeated. Risks to repayment should drive the covenants you select. For example:

- *Seasonal loans*. The risks include cash being used for purposes other than the acquisition of current assets or excessive inventory accumulation or speculation or not being paid out at the start of a normal cleanup period. Covenant selection should focus on the use of proceeds or prohibitions on fixed-asset expenditure and dividends, the debt-to-equity ratio, and the cleanup period or note maturity.
- *Term loans*. The risks include adequacy of cash generation, the addition of competing debt, and sudden business reversals. You should consider such covenants as debt-service coverage, capital expenditure and dividend limitations, prohibitions on new debt, and minimum net worth stepping up over the period of the loan.
- *Bridge loans*. Risks include failure of the take-out event, inadequacy of secondary sources of repayment, and insufficient cash flow for long-term survival. Covenants should focus on maturity of the loan, collateral, and cash flow.
- *Permanent capital loans*. The risks include deterioration of collateral, insufficient cash generation, and use of cash for purposes other than debt repayment. Covenants should focus on borrowing base eligibility, interest coverage, prohibitions on the use of cash, minimum net worth, and debt-to-worth ratio.

The discipline of initially limiting yourself to two or three financial covenants forces you to design efficient and effective covenants without redundancy. For example, if you deduct capital expenditures from cash generation in a debt-service coverage ratio, do you also need to limit capital expenditures? Or if you design an appropriate debt-service covenant, do you also need to limit salaries? You may reasonably end up with more than two or three financial covenants, but after applying this discipline, you should frequently find two or three are sufficient.

Appropriate covenant selection is easier if you have done a good job at logical loan structuring. Isolating the types of loans in terms of repayment tends to highlight the risks and makes it easier to explain necessary covenants to your customer.

How tightly you set covenants is highly judgmental and a function of your assessment of the risk. Do not allow the competition or marketplace to dictate your terms. For example, net worth covenants on many commercial paper backup lines currently are set so low that a company could go into a virtual free fall and drop into noninvestment grade before a bank could do anything about it.

EVENTS OF DEFAULT

You have set covenants based on management's representations to you and have boiled them down to the truly essential. As you craft covenants, you should be thinking about how you will react if they are broken.

If a covenant is violated, determine the cause, reassess your risk rating, and develop a preliminary recommended action plan for discussion with your manager. The problem loan warning bell has rung, and you should drop everything and address the issue. If the violation is "no big deal," you have set your covenants incorrectly or you are procrastinating.

Your manager wants to learn of covenant violations immediately and from you, not the next level of management. Be prepared to review the loan documentation and determine if additional legal review is appropriate. You want to be sure that all documentation is correct, particularly anything relating to collateral and guaranties. If documentation is incorrect, you may now have the leverage to fix it. Many banks have a policy requiring all documents be reviewed by legal counsel when the risk rating drops below a certain point. You also must send a notice of default to your borrower.

After discussing the appropriate course of action with your manager, you should meet with the borrower and negotiate your plan of action, which might be any of the following:

- Acknowledge and waive the event of default. This approach might be reasonable if some unusual and nonrecurring event has caused the violation and there is no fundamental change in risk.
- Restructure the credit. If the risk has changed but is still acceptable, you may negotiate a change in pricing, administration, collateral and guaranties, reporting frequency, and so forth. You also may charge a fee to cover time spent on dealing with the covenant violation.
- Ask the borrower to find another lender. Sometimes the borrower is in total denial and cannot agree that there is a problem. If you have set your covenants appropriately, the borrower should still be attractive to another lender. Set a time limit for moving the loan and demand progress reports. Discussion with other lenders might be a reality check for the borrower and cure the denial. In that case, you may be able to restructure the credit.
- Move the borrower to workout status.

A covenant violation demands a reaction. If you ignore it, you may be establishing a course of dealing for which a court might later hold that you have negated your rights under the agreement. Dealing with a violation also lets the borrower know that an agreement should be taken seriously. You want to impress on your customer that you will react reasonably but that you will always react.

OBJECTIONS

When covenant violations do occur, experienced lenders react reasonably and rationally, balancing both the interests of shareholders and their customers. In practice, covenant violations usually lead to several instances of restructuring before a borrower is asked to leave. Transferring the customer to workout status is a last resort and frequently means you did not react fast enough or the borrower incurred a sudden and unexpected reversal.

Regardless of the rights your documents give you, lender liability issues can arise if you act irrationally. The Golden Rule is not a bad guide. Or put more cynically, as only H.L. Mencken could do it, "Conscience is the inner voice that warns us someone may be looking." A good standard is how would you feel describing your actions to a newspaper reporter or a jury.

When you negotiate with an inexperienced borrower, you are walking a fine line because the borrower may find covenants and events of default intimidating. You also should note that if the borrower is totally unconcerned, you may have a problem. Debt and its consequences should command a certain respect.

You are, in effect, trying to sell a product with a great many warning labels attached. The best approach is to deal with borrower concerns head on. Never try to sugarcoat covenants or dismiss them as "just boilerplate." Your discussion with the borrower might proceed along the following lines:

> Without limiting any rights contained in the final loan agreement, financial covenants are an integral part of that document. The covenants are based on your projections and expectations of the performance of your company and represent our mutual understanding of these expectations. Therefore, we do not view covenants as controls. Rather, we view them as common agreement on the future direction that you will take your company. If conditions change and covenants are breached, we expect that these changes will bring us back together to examine causes and renegotiate the terms of our relationship.
>
> We attempt to limit the number of covenants to the absolute minimum necessary to monitor your company's performance and expect you to

understand them and monitor them yourself. The two principal financial covenants that should be part of our agreement are:

1. Maximum debt-to-worth ratio of 1.4 to 1. This ratio assures us that you, as owners, will maintain a substantial investment in the company in some reasonable relation to the creditors that have more at risk than you do. This leverage ratio is slightly higher than the industry average. Your debt-to-worth ratio is currently 1.28 to 1.
2. Net profit plus depreciation divided by current maturities of long-term debt should not fall below 1.6 to 1. This ratio provides an indication of your ability to service your term debt as it falls due. The ratio of 1.6 to 1 is approximately the average for your industry and for your last four quarters, assuming this additional debt, your ratio would be 1.75 to 1. We will provide you with a form of compliance certificate that you will furnish us periodically and that explains the exact calculation of these ratios.

A borrower should reasonably be concerned with the covenants in a loan agreement. The best way to deal with objections to them is to address them openly and honestly and ensure that there is an understanding of their purpose.

DOCUMENTATION

After negotiating covenants and other details of the transaction, you should prepare, or have prepared, the loan documentation. Documentation has a cost, including legal and filing fees, storage, monitoring, and the time spent reading it by you, the borrower, lawyers, document specialists, administrators, loan review staff, and regulators.

Because of the high cost of documentation, it should reflect the risk and be kept as simple as possible. It can always be redone if the risk changes and you have inserted appropriate covenants.

APPROACH

While consumers have enjoyed some success in pressuring institutions to simplify and use plain English in credit agreements and insurance policies, commercial credit documentation has, if anything, become more complex. There are a number of reasons for this disturbing trend:

- Whenever a new peril or loss is discovered, defensive clauses are incorporated into agreements. Rarely is anything deleted. In a complex and litigious world, new perils are added with increasing frequency, and documentation is enhanced to mitigate new risks.

- Lawyers are paid to protect their clients so when in doubt, they attempt to cover every conceivable base. Bankers become intimidated and go along with what, in many cases, is overkill.
- Lawyers argue that their wording in a document, no matter how convoluted and incomprehensible, has years of precedent and that to change it would be dangerous. It also is true that all the verbiage is in word processors, so documentation can be produced with little thought or effort. Redoing the verbiage would require effort, which takes time.
- Lengthy and arcane documentation generates higher legal fees. This pay-by-the-pound mentality was exacerbated by leveraged transactions in which legal and investment banking fees were packed into closing costs and paid from the loan proceeds.

Simplifying documentation requires doing battle with the internal and external legal establishment, a task that makes the 12 labors of Hercules seem like child's play. It is probably not worth the effort as long as the industry's borrowers accept the status quo. Unfortunately, some organization—no doubt a nonbank competitor—will ultimately develop simplified documentation as a competitive weapon.

Although you should use your bank's preprinted notes, security agreements, guaranty forms, and so forth, you can exercise some creativity in credit or letter agreements. If you have well-selected covenants, there is no need to document 90-95% of your customers for the 5-10% that will deteriorate to the watch list or the 0.5% that will be charged off. If you have the collateral and guaranties you think you have and a well-designed covenant is breached, you effectively have a demand note. What more do you need? You can always restructure your loan at that point and design a new agreement with more verbiage if it adds value.

Excessively lengthy documentation produces problems other than considerable cost. It is difficult and time-consuming to understand, so monitoring compliance becomes erratic. It produces constant violations of insignificant clauses, so the entire document is trivialized. If violations are not acknowledged and waived, you may have a course of dealing issue. Excessive documentation ultimately controls you rather than your borrower.

LAWYERS

Your bank should have a policy on when you need a lawyer to assist you with loan documentation. Such a policy is only a guide and leaves plenty of room for interpretation. Before deciding to bring in a lawyer, you need answers to the following questions:

- Who is the borrower? As obvious as this sounds, many larger enterprises have holding companies with numerous subsidiaries. To analyze a situation like this, you will need an organization chart and consolidating statements to understand where the assets and liabilities are lodged and which entities are generating and using cash.
- What type of legal entity is the borrower? Is it a corporation, general or limited partnership, or sole proprietorship? Under what state laws does it operate?
- What authorizes the borrower to enter into a loan agreement and who is authorized to sign it?
- Are you extending a committed or conditional facility?
- Who will use the funds? Will your borrower relend the proceeds of your loan to a subsidiary? Who will repay the loan?
- Where is the collateral located? Is it in different states? Is it movable?
- Does the collateral include such items as vehicles, aircraft, intangibles, and personal property affixed to real property that have unique filing requirements?
- Do other creditors claim collateral owned by your borrower?
- Is your borrower deteriorating?

If your borrower is a corporation organized in your state and all the collateral consisting of receivables, inventory, and equipment is located in the state as well, you or someone in your bank is probably perfectly competent to document the transaction. As complexity increases, you cross the line and need a lawyer. Ask your manager if the policy is not clear.

If you use a lawyer, your borrower will probably use one, too, so the complexity of managing the relationship increases considerably. A few guidelines should be considered:

- Remember that you are responsible for the relationship with your customer, and you make all business decisions for the bank. Your lawyer's responsibility is to advise you on legal risks.
- Ensure that you are comfortable with collateral filings, guaranty validity, and the enforceability of your note. These are areas in which you most likely will always agree with your lawyer. However, your lawyer may also suggest every covenant that has ever been written. If you have a few well-designed covenants, you should make the business decision to waive the other well-intentioned covenants that add little value.

- Never allow the lawyers to get between you and your customer. Think of what happens in a divorce proceeding. Always negotiate directly with your customer and never permit your message to be carried by anyone else.
- Determine up front who is paying legal fees and ask for an estimate even if your customer is paying. If it is too high, ask for a reduction.
- If your lawyer says something cannot be done, then ask how it can be done.

A lawyer can be a value adding partner in furthering your business relationships or an expensive obstacle to accomplishing results. If the lawyer becomes the latter, try another one. There are plenty out there. Like any true partnership, a good working relationship with your lawyer demands communication, an understanding of responsibilities, and mutual respect.

CLOSING

After all you have done to bring the loan request to this point, the closing may seem anticlimactic, and it should. A good closing is dull and uneventful. A bad closing is exciting.

The purpose of the closing is to provide the bank with all the required documentation and then disburse the loan proceeds appropriately. The closing can be quite simple in documentation and take place in several minutes in your office or by mail with a known customer. Or it can involve a lengthy loan agreement with multiple exhibits, participants, lawyers, and complicated disbursements.

In a complex loan closing, you should prepare a closing agenda and send it to all participants in advance. The agenda sets the time and place of the closing and the estimated completion time. Be sure to conclude early enough to provide ample time for disbursements into different time zones. Also, warn your wire transfer unit.

The agenda should notify each participant what documents they are to bring. You should not close if you fail to receive the requested documents. If participants do not bring the required documents, you have made it their problem by notifying them in the closing agenda. If you disburse funds, then you have made getting the documents your problem.

A complex closing requires thorough planning and orchestration. If complications arise, analyze why they occurred and learn from them. One of the responsibilities of your lawyer is to ensure a smooth closing, and you should work closely with your partner to make sure this happens.

If you are dealing with a new customer, a closing also is an opportune time to review the mutual expectations of borrower and banker discussed in

Chapter 2. The closing can be a bully pulpit, particularly before you have disbursed the loan proceeds.

MONITORING

Once the loan is closed, your task does not end. You now must monitor the loan to ensure that the risk does not change. There are two basic principles of monitoring. First, make sure you have selected a minimum number of well-designed covenants that when breached, signal a real change in risk. Second, enroll your borrower in the monitoring process by ensuring that management understands the agreement and its importance, and that management is responsible for monitoring compliance and reporting violations.

If you have not already discussed compliance reporting with management, the loan closing provides a good opportunity to do so. Any loan or letter agreement that contains covenants also should contain a mechanism for management to report compliance. This reporting should be the borrower's responsibility not the banker's. You can spot-check compliance, but you should not be doing all the calculations for every borrower in your portfolio.

The importance of well-designed covenants becomes obvious when your portfolio is audited by loan review. Many lenders when confronted with a long list of technical exceptions state that they are not important. The obvious response, of course, is, Why did you put them in an agreement if they are not important? Including long lists of well-intentioned trivia into loan agreements eventually strangles you. Remember that the lawyer who recommends doing so does not have to monitor the loan.

When you design covenants with the borrower, you also should discuss computations and reporting with whomever will do the calculations. You can then design a compliance certificate that will be completed periodically by the borrower. Make sure it is understood. A compliance certificate might look like Exhibit 6.1.

Well-crafted covenants and compliance certificates make the borrower your partner in the monitoring process. You should never bear this responsibility and workload alone.

SUMMARY

Once you have obtained internal approval for your customer's loan, you can negotiate the final details including a few well-crafted financial covenants. These covenants are designed to alert you to changes in risk. If a covenant is breached, discuss the cause with your manager and develop an action plan.

EXHIBIT 6.1

COMPLIANCE CERTIFICATE

To: First National Bank Date

Dear Sirs:

In accordance with our Credit Agreement dated _____, attached are our financial statements for the period ending _____. We are in compliance with the financial covenants of the Credit Agreement and the calculations made to determine compliance were the following:

Section 5.1 Debt to Equity

Total liabilities	__________
Total equity	__________
Total liabilities divided by total equity	__________
Agreed maximum	__________

Section 5.2 Debt-Service Coverage

Net profit plus depreciation for last four quarters	__________
Current maturities of long-term debt	__________
Net profit plus depreciation divided by current maturities	__________
Agreed minimum	__________

Section 5.3 Fixed-Asset Expenditures

Year to date fixed-asset expenditure	__________
Agreed maximum	__________

I have further reviewed the Credit Agreement and have no knowledge of the occurrence of any Event of Default or any event that with the passage of time would constitute an Event of Default.

Sincerely,

Title

In preparing the loan documentation, determine if the assistance of a lawyer is necessary. Carefully plan the loan closing with an agenda when several different parties are involved. Never disburse funds until all the documents are in your control. The borrower should become your partner in monitoring the loan once the funds are disbursed with the aid of well-designed compliance certificates.

Chapter 7

Managing the Market

With an active customer base and a list of prospects, you are ready to practice the time management, marketing, and credit disciplines discussed in earlier chapters. However, one step is still missing. If you exercise well-developed skills in a random manner, you will never maximize your opportunities. You must set priorities that focus your energy and talents where they can produce the greatest profit.

Setting priorities involves an understanding of customer profitability, potential, and expectations. If profitability or potential is high, a relationship plan can help guide a coordinated sales effort.

You can enhance efficiency by learning a few techniques and being alert to best practices within the organization and industry. The most productive and profitable bankers learn early that a clean credit portfolio is essential to efficiency. Problem credits demand immediate attention and sidetrack the best marketing efforts.

SETTING PRIORITIES

Before launching an assault on your marketplace, a little careful planning can produce significant results. Your organization should provide you with some basic tools to make the job easier. If these are not available, then you may need to do some improvising.

PROFITABILITY MEASUREMENT

It is very difficult to be in the relationship management business without a tool that describes what a customer does with a bank, that is, the relationship, and measures its profitability. Yet many banks that proclaim they are relationship oriented have no customer profitability system—a contradiction in terms.

Whether your bank buys a system or creates its own, the system inevitably becomes embroiled in at least three controversies:

1. The allocation of overhead.

2. The allocation of capital.

3. The assignment of accurate costs to products and services.

The dialogue is worthwhile up to a point. Participants gain a much better understanding of the balance sheet and income statement. They learn that overhead expenses do not just go away and that some products are losing money no matter what costs are assumed.

At some point, however, management must conclude the dialogue and make some basic decisions. These decisions will make few people happy because they affect perceived profitability of the departments involved. The perfect is the enemy of the good, and while you can never attain the perfect system, a good one can produce remarkable results.

A good customer profitability system may not equate exactly to the general ledger. Does it really matter if it is off by 5-10%? It is not an accounting system; it is a system that captures what a customer is doing with the bank and what profit it is generating. These data can be sliced many different and useful ways, such as profitability by customer, branch, banker, and product.

When a customer profitability system is combined with sales tracking, then managers and bankers really have something to talk to each other about. Managers have a basis for setting workload standards and sales objectives, while bankers have a tool for prioritizing their efforts, truly a win-win situation.

If your bank does not have a customer profitability or sales tracking system, you can design your own by making some simple assumptions on net interest margin, provision for loan loss, overhead, and so forth. For noncredit services, you should be able to find a gross revenue number, and the product provider can help you derive a rough profit margin. You can track your own customer and prospect calling activities and results.

Although this rough approximation of profitability may not be particularly accurate, it will rank order customers if applied consistently. This ordering of profitability is highly useful in setting priorities and may give your bank some impetus to adopt a standardized system.

PROFIT POTENTIAL

A rank order of your customers by profitability gives you some idea of an appropriate priority for calls. How you factor in prospect calls depends, to some extent, on the wallet share of your customers. In other words, if you have low product penetration in your customer base, it makes sense to weight your calling efforts heavier on the customer side.

As you call on customers and prospects, try to determine their profit potential by finding out what products and services they are qualified for that you offer. The easiest way is to ask them. Most people have no problem telling you what financial services they are buying, from whom, and for how much. They also are qualified for products and services that they are not buying because they have never heard of them or think they are unsuitable.

Determining profit potential takes time but can focus your efforts significantly. As you explore this potential, look for natural openings, such as contract expirations, when it would be appropriate to display your wares.

What you ultimately want to determine for your customers and prospects is the annual profit potential if you had 100% of the business your bank could fulfill. With customer profitability and customer and prospect potential established, you are well on your way to prioritizing your marketplace. One additional piece of information is necessary.

PARTNER OR VENDOR

Your relationship with a customer can be described as falling somewhere on a scale between partner and vendor. Where you fall on the scale reflects the customer's management style and expectations of you. You may not learn your position immediately. It may take a number of calls and sales attempts.

At the partner end of the scale, you and your customer have open and candid communications that begin at the planning table at which you share strategies. The banker is considered a trusted advisor who adds value by being responsive to needs as well as bringing new ideas. The bank and the customer have multiple levels of contact and problems are surfaced and solved at low levels in both organizations. The customer does not hesitate to suggest product development ideas to the bank.

Because the bank is at the planning table with the customer, the bank sees sales opportunities first. The bank must be competitive but can achieve reasonable pricing, which acknowledges the responsiveness and quality of service. The bank normally gets the nod in a competitive tie or close call. At the same time, the bank frankly states when it cannot be competitive on a particular product or provide quality service.

At the vendor end of the scale, the customer sees no value to a relationship approach. The customer views the bank as one of a number of sources providing unbundled products and services. Cost is the primary concern, and quality may not be much of a consideration. The customer generally initiates sales opportunities, and they are usually in the form of an invitation to bid. Unless the ground rules are well established, the bank might find its bid and ideas shopped to other competitors.

Obviously, placing your relationship with a customer on a partner/vendor scale is highly judgmental. Nevertheless, it is also quite useful. Using the information you have gathered on customer profitability, profit potential, and partner/vendor position, you can place each customer in the grid in Exhibit 7.1. Select the appropriate box by partner/vendor position and profitability and after the customer's name, put the potential profit in parenthesizes.

Of course, you want every customer in the upper right box but will probably find they are well scattered. Upon reflection, you may conclude that your chances of moving customers from a vendor to a partner type of relationship are limited. You would need to change management styles or expectations of you, which is not easy. On the other hand, without appropriate communications and attention, customers might readily change you from a partner to a vendor. This demotion can happen in times of easy money when desperate competitors commoditize bank offerings.

As you study the grid, it should become obvious that spreading your time evenly over your customer base is highly inefficient, if not stupid. Yet many bankers still take the same vendor-oriented customers to the golf outings year after year when all that is necessary is an annual call to ensure they still have the bank's number on their rolodexes.

Both partner and vendor relationships can be necessary and contribute to the profitability of your bank. They should just be handled differently. Use the grid to help prioritize your time and resources and improve your profitability.

Also, study the grid to find out how vulnerable you are to the 80/20 rule, that is, where 80% of your profits are accounted for by 20% of your customers. The results tend to focus your calling efforts and underscore how vulnerable many commercial banking portfolios are.

RELATIONSHIP PLANS

With priorities based on profitability, potential, and partner/vendor position, you are in a good position to manage your market efficiently. The relationship plan is a useful tool in meeting your objectives.

A relationship plan simply outlines what you will attempt to accomplish with selected customers and prospects during the forthcoming year. It will be

EXHIBIT 7.1

CUSTOMER PROFITABILITY PROFILE

Past 12 months net after-tax profit	<$10,000	$10–$20,000	$20–$30,000	$30,000+
Valued Partner • At the planning table • Shared strategies • Trusted advisor • Multiple levels of contact • Little competitive pressure				
Partner • Multifaceted relationship • Occasional surprises • More subject to competition				
Valued Vendor • Several products sold • Quality considered • Competitive within a select group of providers				
Vendor • One or two products • Price is key • Not quality oriented • Bids widely solicited • May shop proposals or ideas				

brief—one or two pages—as your efforts should be directed toward planning and coordinating not writing. A plan serves to gather the resources of the organization and direct them to a target. For example, a plan might include a joint call with senior management, a meeting with a cash management technician, an invitation to a seminar on international trade finance, and a lunch with a human resources specialist to discuss employee benefit programs. Such a plan requires coordination and agreement with all participants and a mechanism for follow up. Your manager and all participants in the plan should, of course, receive a copy.

Relationship plans are powerful tools in focusing coordinated sales efforts, and they are invaluable to the sales manager. However, too much of a good thing can destroy their effectiveness. You should probably prepare no more than 10 annually on a staggered basis. If you are required to do too many, it becomes an exercise in meeting paper deadlines rather than a powerful planning tool. If it is done at one time during the year rather than on a staggered basis, you and your manager will be overwhelmed with process and paper.

ENHANCING EFFICIENCY

To manage your market effectively, you should always look for tools and techniques that can make you more effective and the job more enjoyable. The alert manager also is searching for best practices to share with subordinates. The following ideas might be helpful.

CALLING AGENDAS

Sales managers find calling agendas quite useful in quality control and follow-up. They help ensure that calls are planned rather than public relations exercises. Bankers find that they add professionalism and allow the customer to participate, which often results in a new sales idea.

A calling agenda can be a simple letter confirming the meeting and setting forth the topics to be covered. It should give the customer a chance to make revisions that might result in sales opportunities. A calling agenda might look like Exhibit 7.2.

Calling agendas are not appropriate for every call, particularly when the purpose is well known such as the negotiation of loan covenants. They are, however, quite useful on sales calls. They give the customer the opportunity to bring in other interested decision makers or influencers. Calling agendas tend to ensure planning and a copy to the manager improves the sales management process.

COMMUNICATIONS

Once you have prioritized your customers and prospects and established a reasonable calling frequency, you may find, depending on the nature of your portfolio, that you just cannot get to everyone. An asset-based loan administrator may have 12 to 15 accounts. A commercial banker in a branch may have 100.

Maintaining some periodic communication with your entire customer and prospect base is desirable and helps ensure that you get a call when an opportunity arises. Keeping in touch requires a good tickler system as a reminder. Look for occasions that take little time, such as a telephone call, mailing an article of mutual interest with a handwritten note on your card, and sending a birthday greeting. In addition, your manager might hold an annual open house to bring customers and prospects into the bank. With a little ingenuity, you can

EXHIBIT 7.2

SAMPLE CALLING AGENDA

Mr. John B. Wolf
President
Construction Supply Company

Dear Jack:

I look forward to seeing you at your office on Tuesday, January 24 at 9:30 a.m. Joining me will be Judy Roberts, manager of our human resources department, and John Blake, employee benefits administration. Their cards are enclosed. As we discussed, I would like them to give you and Pat Millner a brief overview of how a 401K plan can give you a competitive edge in salary administration. This discussion should take about 20 minutes after which I would suggest that Pat, Judy, and John meet separately to go over the details.

You and I can then discuss your year-end results, projections, and financial needs for the coming year. I also would like to make you aware of a new technique to enhance credit quality of your foreign sales and speed up collection. We should finish by 10:30 a.m.

If you have other thoughts, call me or jot them down on this letter and fax it back to me.

Sincerely,

easily maintain communications with your lower priority market base and let them know you care.

PRODUCT SPECIALISTS

Although many banks profess to be in relationship management, few have truly clarified the roles of the relationship manager and product specialists. The unfortunate controversies frequently boil down to the question of who owns the customer. At its best, the relationship manager brings to bear all the resources of the organization to tailor mutually profitable solutions for the customer. The relationship manager acts as a facilitator but knows when to stand back and let the product specialist take over. This arrangement is possible because of mutual trust and understanding of capabilities.

At its worst, the relationship manager is a gatekeeper jealously guarding access to the customer. There is little trust between the relationship manager and product specialists, so the manager wants to be present at every customer contact to ensure that the specialist does not cause irreparable damage. There is no understanding of how far a manager should take the sale and when the specialist should be called. There are interminable arguments over the allocation of costs and profits. Employees become internally focused rather than directing their efforts to the marketplace.

Arriving at a culture that balances the roles of relationship managers and product specialists in favor of the customer is management's responsibility. Nevertheless, you must make the most of the environment in which you find yourself. As a novice commercial banker, you might consider the first sale and closing of a product a training experience and follow it through to completion with the product specialist. You can then develop an understanding of the appropriate time to hand your customer off to the specialist.

Ideally, you want to establish multilevel contacts between your bank and the customer, so problems and opportunities are dealt with efficiently at the appropriate level. If you act as a gatekeeper, then every problem the customer has with the bank is your responsibility. Not only is this highly inefficient, but soon your relationship with the customer is poisoned by dealing with countless problems.

The alert manager understands the value of appropriate role definition and discusses issues at sales meetings to assess the state of the culture. The manager also understands the role overdeveloped egos can play in unnecessary gatekeeping and coaches and counsels those who need it.

BEST PRACTICES

One of the best ways of learning efficiency enhancing techniques is to watch what others are doing in and outside your organization and appropriate and modify the best practices. You will probably notice that some of the best sales results come from referrals that should be carefully cultivated. Ask your good customers and opinion leaders for referrals. When you get a referral, do not ignore the rules of etiquette. Follow up immediately and be sure to keep the referring party informed. The giver of a referral is taking a chance on you and expects acknowledgment. Do not disappoint this potential source of business.

Your manager should have established a mechanism for circulating copies of correspondence and file comments. This circulating file not only keeps coworkers informed but also serves as a source for best practices. Watch for especially well-written letters, proposals, and file comments and learn from them. Good file comments are brief and to the point. Unfortunately, some individuals spend as much time writing about calls as they do in front of the customer.

Working in a team environment provides an excellent opportunity to learn from the best. It also provides for the opposite result, so practice some discernment.

CREDIT RISK

Few events are more time-consuming than problem credits. They set their own priorities and require you to drop everything you are doing. They rarely improve with age, so if you procrastinate, you will find that they consume even more of your time. You will never manage your market effectively if you must deal with many problem credits.

The best commercial bankers have had experience with problem credits and know firsthand the toll they can take. Consequently, they tend to avoid the quick sales hits in favor of working an active pipeline of attractive, long-term prospects. They realize that there is no compensation for excessive risk. They also tend to have the most profitable portfolios.

New bankers want to get on the scoreboard and tend to view risk much more optimistically. Although this thinking is understandable, it can cause unintended results several years later. In commercial lending, there is a long lag time between cause and effect. As a result, review your prospects and pending loan transactions with your manager and listen to words of caution. You will never truly understand risk and reward until you have been a lender through an entire business cycle.

You also should watch very closely for the financial and nonfinancial signals that indicate a problem credit in your portfolio. Because banking experience has been so cyclically devastating, much has been written on problem loan identification and handling. Read it and take heed.

Your biggest problem may well be denial, so it pays to know yourself. Account officers often regard problem credits as assaults on their egos rather than statistical inevitabilities. This viewpoint leads to procrastination and worse problems later. If you even suspect you have a problem developing, talk to your manager. Take advantage of the experience available to you.

The most profitable and effective managers of their markets are not the bankers who take big credit risks. Rather, the best bankers tend to have very clean portfolios. They operate in a consistent, disciplined manner and produce results evenly over time. Learn from them.

SUMMARY

Managing your market effectively requires setting priorities based on your understanding of customer profitability, potential, and expectations of you and your bank. You need a good customer profitability and sales tracking system along with other tools such as the relationship plan.

To enhance your efficiency, you must learn a number of techniques such as the use of calling agendas and role definition with product specialists. Effectiveness in the marketplace requires a clean loan portfolio because problem credits are all absorbing. The most profitable and efficient bankers have a very clear understanding of risk and reward.

Chapter 8

Managing Internally

Companies survive and prosper because they are externally focused. They listen to their customers and respond to their needs. They seek ways to add value and, in doing so, build sustainable competitive advantages.

Banks have no monopoly on products and services. Most banking products and services can be copied in very short order. Skilled people can be hired. What distinguishes one bank from another is an external focus on its marketplace and a caring attitude by all employees. In short, execution.

If your organization is internally focused, management has a serious problem that it must resolve. If you are internally focused, you have the ability to change course.

You cannot be successful in commercial banking unless you direct your energies and talents toward the customer. At the same time, you must balance customer and shareholder needs while managing your internal relationships.

To manage internally, you need to become comfortable with the organization, learn from it, contribute to it, and use its resources to help you in the marketplace. Without becoming excessively oriented towards internal issues, you should learn, nevertheless, to manage your role in the performance evaluation, mentoring, and skill and career development.

PERFORMANCE EVALUATION

Theoretically, the performance appraisal should benefit everyone. It should point out strengths and weaknesses and show the recipient how to improve. It should raise issues of concern and point out opportunities or challenges that management is emphasizing and that further the objectives of the organization. It should offer ideas on career development. Unfortunately, it rarely succeeds at any of these goals.

ADDRESSING PROBLEMS

Few corporate practices are as universally disliked as the annual performance appraisal. Surveys of supervisors and employees across a broad range of industries rate it a failure. It has, however, been a bonanza for consultants called into organizations to install new procedures and forms. Within a short period of time, participants usually become disenchanted with the new systems.

Managers are confronted with a yearly deadline that they know will ruin several weekends. As most organizations grow flatter, the number of appraisals managers must write and give increases, and the paper burden becomes immense. Attention shifts from the customer to the internal process.

Without minimum performance standards and carefully thought-out objectives tailored to individual requirements, a good performance evaluation is impossible. No one likes to deliver negative feedback, particularly if it cannot be substantiated. It may be justified, but it will probably not be delivered if it will just provoke contention.

Consequently, there is a tendency to overrate individuals as managers understandably attempt to avoid controversy. Organizations have turned in terrible performance or have ceased to exist while the average numerical performance rating for its employees is quite high.

Overrating feeds on itself because a "good" rating is usually interpreted internally as "lousy." Because employees know that a rating no better than good affects their pay and think it also means a slow career death, they will push ratings higher. Then when managers needs to terminate someone for poor performance, they discover to their horror that the individual has been rated good or better in the past.

Performance appraisals are often joined with salary actions. As a result, the employee tends to be more focused on the potential increase than his or her performance evaluation. It is not easy for a manager to discuss career planning with someone who at that moment is more interested in what will be in the next paycheck.

CREATING A COOPERATIVE EFFORT

Performance evaluation should be a cooperative effort in which both the manager and the employee participate. If minimum standards have not been established for the job, then you can establish your own as discussed in Chapter 3. These standards should revolve around such activities as credit quality, sales, profit, workload, and customer satisfaction. Then establish three to five specific objectives that you will attempt to accomplish during the year.

These objectives should focus on areas you need to strengthen or areas that the organization is emphasizing.

Review these standards and objectives with your manager who may very well modify them. They should then be the basis for mutual expectations of performance and accomplishments. On a quarterly basis, you can prepare a memo for your manager summarizing your performance against standards and objectives. This memo can be the basis for informal discussion and feedback.

Setting minimum standards and individual objectives is normally the job of the manager, but if they do not exist, there is no reason why you should not help out. Doing so not only assists the manager in accomplishing the job it also sets mutual expectations and provides a logical method of evaluating performance. If administering standards and objectives is accomplished during the year and supplemented with informal coaching and counseling, the performance appraisal is easy to write and almost an anticlimax.

HANDLING CONFLICT

If you are surprised or disagree with what you hear in a performance evaluation, do not become defensive or combative. After all, maybe you really are arrogant, cynical, or whatever might be said about you. Your evaluation is a time to listen to what your manager is saying, is not saying, and wants to say.

Performance comparisons with standards and objectives should be relatively straightforward. There may be extenuating circumstances, and you should be prepared to document them. Highly subjective opinions, which are just as important but impossible to document, should be heeded. Managers are generally careful about negative feedback knowing that it will cause controversy. Frequently, they will ignore it to avoid the stress. Silence is not doing you a favor because negative impressions are not forgotten.

If you receive highly subjective negative feedback, ask to be informed on the spot when the behavior is noted in the future. This way, you can understand the issue and correct it as it occurs, which is what coaching and counseling is all about. Make note of areas to be strengthened or behaviors that need changing and follow up on a periodic basis with your manager to see if progress is being made or if you are in agreement. If appropriate, suggest additional training or other courses of action.

If you receive an overall rating with which you disagree, ask what is expected to achieve the higher rating. Should the response be vague, there many be a lack of standards. You might ask to put together a list of standards or expectations for mutual discussion. The point is to participate actively in resolution rather than to become sullen or combative.

Every organization has its own rhythms such as budgeting, salary and promotion cycles, board meetings, and examinations. Should you feel compelled to discuss salary or promotion with your manager, do so before salary budgets are started or promotion lists are compiled. If the facts are unclear, ask what the qualifications for promotion are rather than express a demand. Discussing these issues outside of the normal cycles puts additional pressure on the manager. Although the manager may agree with you, he or she could be reluctant to make an exception that would have to be defended to the organizational hierarchy.

Improving the Process

What can you expect in an environment that values developing its human resources? The development of people is part of a manager's job description and compensation, not an afterthought once the numbers are hit. The manager should have clear standards in place for minimum performance expectations and negotiate objectives with employees that address weaknesses and run with strengths. On a quarterly basis, the employee should update the manager on performance standards and objectives. The manager should provide positive and negative feedback on a continuing basis as behavioral events occur. These coaching and counseling sessions are brief and given and received in the spirit of improving performance. The annual performance appraisal is a summation of the year's progress and contains no surprises.

When the developmental and performance evaluation process is poor, it is often caused by lack of emphasis on the part of senior management. Many senior managements focus only on the tangible, which translates to "Hit your numbers and get a clean audit." Yet these same managements know that in a highly competitive environment in which no one has a monopoly on products and services, it is the intangible that distinguishes organizations and produces sustainable competitive advantages.

The intangibles include quality and customer satisfaction nurtured by caring and well-coached employees focusing externally on their marketplace. Management recognizes these intangibles by saying, "People are our most important asset." This assertion often provokes smirks and derision among the employees. If it were true, then why are managers rewarded only for hitting their numbers and not for developing their people?

To have a meaningful focus on the intangible, management must believe that hitting the numbers, as important as that is, is not the only element of a manager's job description. The development of people, quality, and customer satisfaction also is the responsibility of managers even if these factors cannot be measured perfectly.

To ingrain the intangibles into an organization's culture and belief system, senior management must make them part of the manager's appraisal process and compensation. Senior management must inspect what it expects. Inspection would include meaningful reviews of appraisals written by managers, "two down" lunches at which senior management communicates with a manager's employees, training in coaching, counseling, and feedback, and more.

Unless senior management believes that intangibles are part of a manager's job description and incorporates them into the rewards system, nothing will change. The performance evaluation process will still be unsatisfactory and all the new procedures and forms brought in by consultants will fail.

Although you can recognize what a good developmental system should entail, you can do little to change the process. That is the job of the corner office and senior management. You can, however, make a difference between you and your manager by playing a meaningful, cooperative role in your developmental process.

MENTORS

In many performance appraisals, it is what you do not hear that is important. Your manager may have concerns that are highly subjective and withhold them because they cannot be quantified or because giving negative feedback is just too unpleasant.

Say you are participating in a meeting at which everyone is contributing ideas to a colleague who is discussing a loan proposal. If your manager thinks you are being sarcastic and impeding the exchange of views, you need to know about it. This is important, and you need immediate feedback. You would hope that your manager would pull you aside after the meeting and discuss how your behavior might affect the quality of a team environment.

If the manager does give you immediate feedback, take heed. It would not be said if there were not a concern. React positively by saying you appreciate the feedback and ask to be informed immediately if it ever occurs again. Hearing it once out of context at the annual appraisal time is not helpful.

Avoid anger and denial. That is a sure way of shutting off future feedback. If you disagree, ask someone else who cares about you, such as a friend, spouse, sibling, or parent. You may find that others think you are sarcastic as well. A third-party opinion can be a powerful developmental tool. As Robert Burns said more than two hundred years ago:

Oh wad some power the giftie gie us
To see oursels as others see us!

A mentor can do that without lapsing into a Scottish dialect.

ROLE OF THE MENTOR

A mentor is a wise and trusted counselor who is higher up in the organization and more experienced than you. The mentor is someone who takes an interest in your career and sincerely wants to help you on an altruistic basis. Although most mentorships are established informally, some companies do have formal programs.

Your manager could serve as a mentor, although it should probably be someone else. The mentor relationship is subtle and may occur without your recognizing it. It tends to fade away when it is no longer useful. You can do well in an organization without ever having a mentor, although in hindsight, you may have had one or more without recognizing the relationship as such.

A mentor can advise you on the complexities of dealing with the organization, make you known to management, offer opinions on career opportunities, or help on specific issues such as a proposal. And if you are truly fortunate, a mentor can act as a mirror and show you how others see you.

SUBJECTIVE ISSUES

Over the years, I have heard a number of criticisms of employees, and I agreed with many of them. However, many were discussed only obliquely, if at all, with individuals because they were subjective and not quantifiable. On the other hand, many were discussed with individuals who chose not to listen. The following is a partial list of criticisms. You can see how difficult it would be to discuss them unless you enjoy an environment in which feedback is expected and acknowledged.

- Cynical.
- Lazy.
- Uses embarrassingly poor grammar.
- Dresses unprofessionally.
- Arrogant.
- Poor writing ability.
- Bad oral and written presentations.
- Not a team player.

- Sexist, racist, or offensive.
- Sarcastic.
- Looks down on administrative and clerical help.
- Political.
- Surly.
- Poor personal hygiene.
- Aloof.
- Self-centered.
- Talks when should be listening.
- Poor table manners.

Most people are quite surprised when they are told any of the above. It may not be significant, or even true, but perception can become reality and make a difference. If known, these issues can be addressed and cured. One of the roles of a mentor is to point out problem areas and recommend solutions.

ADDITIONAL SKILLS

Continuing education is critical to career success. Although most commercial lenders are given fairly intensive training at the entry level, continuing education is often a random event, at best. Bankers need periodic retreading in the basics as well as exposure to new or evolving techniques and issues.

Don't count on your organization to provide additional training routinely. However, your manager should react positively to training requests that further the bank's objectives. You should be prepared to initiate such requests.

A number of important skills are not always trained because there is often a presumption that you know them or they cannot be taught. These skills are essential to any career direction not just commercial banking.

ORAL AND WRITTEN SKILLS

Good oral and written skills are nothing more than selling or persuasion carried out in some form of presentation. Credit write-ups, discussions with the credit committee, and proposals to customers are all so common to banking you would think that oral and written skills would be routinely included in training programs. They are not.

Your planning, analytical, and persuasive abilities are never so exposed as in an oral or written presentation. As frightening as this may be, speech and writing is a reflection of the way you think. The best way to learn good oral presentation habits is to be coached by professionals using videotape. Although this training can be stressful, it is highly effective because you see and hear yourself as others do and receive immediate feedback. That is what good coaching is all about.

Written skills are best taught by similar coaching. Try to find someone who will take the time to go over examples of your work with you and make suggestions line by line and paragraph by paragraph. This is painstaking work and may be best accomplished by a professional.

Observe the presentations skills of others. Whenever you are particularly impressed or persuaded, dissect the style to discover the reasons why. Learn from the best and reject the rest. There will be plenty of the latter.

ARTISANSHIP

In practicing their art, commercial bankers leave lots of evidence by which they can be judged, including the state of their credit files, length of the past-due and overdraft list, technical exceptions, and attention to deadlines. Descriptive adjectives range from professional, skillful, and competent to sloppy, lazy, and uncaring. You know where you want to be considered on this scale. Pay attention to your artisanship. You can be sure others will.

INTERPERSONAL SKILLS

Whether it is in a business, social, or family setting, good interpersonal skills are at the heart of making the relationship flourish. Good skills can be taught and learned. Bad ones can be overcome. A manager, mentor, spouse, sibling, friend, or parent can provide coaching and counseling. Probably all have tried at one time or another. An open and receptive mind is required. There are useful books and seminars that can complement good coaching. Some of the interpersonal skills you should work on include:

- Negotiating.
- Interviewing.
- Selling.
- Conveying unpleasant information.
- Networking.
- Working as part of a team.
- Giving and receiving feedback.
- Listening.

CAREER DEVELOPMENT

Most banks are quite passive about career development, and many employees seem unaware that their careers are chiefly their own responsibility. This is not a bad arrangement as it leaves your destiny in your own hands. It also reduces the sources of blame.

Companies rarely have grand plans for their employees. Forecasting needs, opportunities, and direction of the industry is virtually impossible. However, if you cannot predict the future, you should at least be flexible enough to react to it. Flexibility requires an available pool of competent, growing people willing to take prudent risks. Companies stagnate not because they cannot see opportunities but because they do not have the human resources to take advantage of them.

Instead of attempting to plot individual careers, senior management should focus on careful selection, training and development, and nurturing a learning environment in which employees can maximize their potential. If management provides that kind of environment, it is your responsibility to take advantage of it. Doing so benefits you and the organization.

A successful career is a combination of many factors including hard work, planning, development, experience, judgment, timing, and luck. Fortunately, careers are long, three or four decades, allowing plenty of time for mistakes, dead ends, second thoughts, and fresh starts. Skills can be learned quickly; translating them into competency takes much longer. The seasoning of a commercial banker requires at least a business cycle.

One mistake individuals commonly make about careers is to be so focused on the future that they forget about mastering the present. If the company cannot predict its future needs, you probably cannot either. While you should always be planning for the future, developing competency and mastering your current position is always the first order of business. Competency is not in abundant supply. Anyone exhibiting competency will be noticed and find that options start opening for the future.

While achieving competency in your current position, look around you and observe how careers are developing in your own organization and the industry. Years ago, commercial banking was the accepted route to senior management. As organizations became flatter and the industry began moving from banking to a broader mission of financial services, career paths of senior management became less clear. Senior managers today have made many seemingly lateral moves to run different kinds of businesses. They have been responsible for creating tangible results in markets. To accomplish these results, they have been willing to change locations and take risks.

At some point in your career, you need to determine to what positions you aspire, how you get there, and if you are willing to pay the price. There are lifestyle trade-offs to consider and questions of achieving a balance between professional and personal life that is appropriate for you.

Also, examine broad changes in your environment. Commercial lending is evolving as the economy and those serving it change. As manufacturing decreases while service and technology oriented firms increase, the demand for traditional commercial loans changes and perhaps diminishes.

Competition is altering commercial lending. Once, only large, stock-exchange-traded companies had access to public markets; now, smaller and smaller companies are refinancing in the debt and equity arena. Securitization and loan pooling are making further inroads into commercial lending.

On the smaller side of commercial businesses, credit-scoring through the retail side of the organization is assuming an increasing role. If credit-scoring is successful, it will not be long before nonbank competition with less overhead enters this market.

There will always be a need for the tailored solutions provided companies by commercial lenders. However, this segment may be eroded by retail techniques such as credit-scoring on the smaller end and public markets and new financing techniques on the larger end. If the segment becomes smaller, it will also become riskier.

Commercial banking of the past is dead. The industry is moving into a much broader range of financial services because of deregulation, nonbank competition, and demographic changes. This evolution creates more businesses under the umbrella of financial services and more opportunities for individuals willing to accept new challenges.

Anyone aspiring to senior management must learn the consumer business as well as the commercial. Although there are many similarities and common skill requirements, the consumer business targets mass markets as opposed to individual companies within a defined market. Consumer managers typically supervise significantly more employees than commercial managers and must be very process oriented. This requires learning different management skills.

The consumer business will no longer be just credit and deposits. As the population ages and borrows less, banks must play a role in assisting customers in wealth creation. Banks must integrate trust departments, investment products, brokerage, and deposit gathering into a wealth creation strategy before the mutual funds own it all.

If wealth continues to polarize with a growing number of rich and poor and a diminishing middle class in between, banks may need to look down scale as well as up scale. Financial institutions of the future will have a much broader view of their marketplace.

Although no one can predict the future, the changes in financial services are dramatically real. The chances of your organization existing in the same form and with the same ownership in the next 5 to 10 years are not great. That certainly has been the case in the last 5 to 10 years. To survive and enjoy a rewarding career in financial services, you must keep expanding your skills through continued education and remain flexible and adaptable.

SUMMARY

Commercial lending is an excellent place to start a career in financial services. It is the most subtle and difficult business to learn. You must navigate between customer needs and your interpretation of the ambiguities of bank policy. The skill requirements are enormous, ranging from the technical to the interpersonal.

Unlike other forms of lending, there are no cookie-cutter solutions that can be pulled out of a drawer to solve a problem. The commercial banker must tailor a solution through face-to-face negotiation using all the expertise acquired through years of training, apprenticeship, and experience. The banker creates a product that bears the stamp of an artisan. Mastering the craft is an art that will serve as a spring board to greater opportunity.

Appendix

Management Practices Questionnaire

I have suggested in this book that bankers learn self-management skills that can, in turn, assist their managers and further the goals of the organization. Management should be a joint effort directed at improving performance.

In addition to the specific issues discussed, managers might use this book in two ways. First, to improve individual performance and, second, to enhance the effectiveness of the unit as a whole.

To improve individual performance, the manager can highlight areas of concern and then give the book to the individual banker suggesting that the highlighted points need discussion. This approach is reasonably nonthreatening and should be used in a coaching spirit that will be helpful to the recipient. I have tried to include most of the areas that, in my experience, bankers could improve.

To enhance the effectiveness of the unit as a whole, the manager can adapt the following questionnaire to suit the particular needs of his or her unit. As the questionnaire covers issues that were discussed in this book, the manager may wish to create a more comprehensive list by reviewing the appendices of *Effective Loan Management* and *Commercial Loan Portfolio Management*, both published by RMA. Chapter 10 of *Effective Loan Management* discusses the use of questionnaires and methods of managing change.

Managers using the questionnaire should have thick skins and realize that high scores in all areas are far from typical. The results can provide an excellent forum for open discussion and strategies for improvement.

The questions are grouped into specific categories of management practices. They are designed to help evaluate the current state of these practices and assist in the establishment of priorities for improvement.

To the right of each question is a blank space in which to evaluate the effectiveness of your organization in dealing with that particular issue. Participants should assign a rating of 1 to 5 as follows:

1. The issue has not been addressed or is handled in a clearly unacceptable manner.
2. The issue is being handled in a barely acceptable manner. Performance is uneven and improvement is needed.
3. The issue is being handled in a reasonably adequate manner, and performance is consistent and generally good. Minimum standards are met.
4. The issue is being handled in a superior manner and standards are generally exceeded.
5. The issue is handled exceptionally well and standards are always exceeded. Performance is always outstanding and provides a best practice or an excellent example to emulate.

Participants also should assess the urgency of the issue by suggesting priorities for change.

Evaluations obviously will be subjective, unless specific standards have been developed for the issue in question. A certain amount of subjectivity does not diminish the value of the exercise. However, ask participants to be as objective as possible, understanding that the purpose is not to achieve a certain raw score but to establish efforts and priorities for improving performance. You may wish to conduct the exercise annually to evaluate progress.

The best results are probably achieved by administering this questionnaire anonymously. You may wish to have participants involved in the compilation of the questionnaire, and you may add space for general comments. Feedback should be given to participants, not only to keep them involved but also to provide a useful step in planning and implementing change.

	Evaluation (1 to 5)	Priority for Change (Use check or X) High	Deferred	Indefinite
A. Loan Administration				
1. Is the written loan policy useful?	_____	_____	_____	_____
2. Is management, the line, and credit in agreement on the types of loans that are to be made within the market?	_____	_____	_____	_____
3. Is the unwritten loan policy well understood?	_____	_____	_____	_____
4. Are there open discussions of credit to enhance training and solidify loan policy?	_____	_____	_____	_____
5. Is there a process for deciding to exit or remain with a deteriorating credit?	_____	_____	_____	_____
6. Is there a policy for how far the bank will go in asset-based lending before the credit is handed off to professionals?	_____	_____	_____	_____
7. Does the bank have an overadvance policy?	_____	_____	_____	_____
8. Does the bank spread the credit write-ups over the year as opposed to concentrating the workload in the spring?	_____	_____	_____	_____
9. Does the credit approval process accomplish its intended objectives?	_____	_____	_____	_____
10. Is there a policy for when lawyers are used and who pays the fees?	_____	_____	_____	_____
11. Do borrowers typically monitor their own loans through compliance certificates?	_____	_____	_____	_____

	Evaluation (1 to 5)	Priority for Change (Use check or X)		
		High	Deferred	Indefinite
A. Loan Administration				
12. Is there an efficient process for approving material changes to credits that have been approved?	_____	_____	_____	_____
13. Have any correlations between debt-service and leverage ratios and risk ratings been developed?	_____	_____	_____	_____
14. Is the credit write-up format efficient and logical?	_____	_____	_____	_____
15. Is there a policy for obtaining legal reviews of watch-listed credits?	_____	_____	_____	_____
16. Have watch-list limits been established and incorporated into performance evaluation?	_____	_____	_____	_____
18. Is the delegation of loan authority reasonable?	_____	_____	_____	_____
19. Are loans consistently broken down into the four types in terms of repayment and structured accordingly?	_____	_____	_____	_____
Category A average ______				
B. Sales Culture				
1. Do bankers receive sales and product training?	_____	_____	_____	_____
2. Have workload standards been set that include customer and prospect calls, expected sales, and referrals.	_____	_____	_____	_____
3. Is the sales management process effective?	_____	_____	_____	_____
4. Are effective sales meetings held?	_____	_____	_____	_____

	Evaluation (1 to 5)	Priority for Change (Use check or X)		
		High	Deferred	Indefinite
B. Sales Culture				
5. Is there training in handling objections?	_____	_____	_____	_____
6. Are relationship plans used on major customers and prospects?	_____	_____	_____	_____
7. Are calls routinely scripted?	_____	_____	_____	_____
8. Does the bank use the telephone for qualifying a market?	_____	_____	_____	_____
9. Do relationship managers hand a prospect off to a technician at the appropriate point?	_____	_____	_____	_____
10. Is there an appropriate mix between customer and prospect calls?	_____	_____	_____	_____
11. Is there a process for tracking the pipeline of new business?	_____	_____	_____	_____
13. Are calling agendas routinely used?	_____	_____	_____	_____
14. Are the roles of relationship managers and product specialists well defined?	_____	_____	_____	_____
15. Is there a standard briefing process for the manager and senior management when calling on customers or prospects?	_____	_____	_____	_____
16. Is there communication with the purchasing department on mutual customers and vendors?	_____	_____	_____	_____
17. Is the organization externally focused on customers and prospects?	_____	_____	_____	_____
18. Is there a useful customer profitability system in place?	_____	_____	_____	_____

	Evaluation (1 to 5)	Priority for Change (Use check or X) High	Deferred	Indefinite
B. Sales Culture				
19. Is there an effective sales tracking system in place?	_____	_____	_____	_____
20. Is the bank profitability vulnerable to the 80/20 rule?	_____	_____	_____	_____
21. Is there a process for propagating best practices?	_____	_____	_____	_____
22. Can market and wallet share be quantified and tied to individual responsibility?	_____	_____	_____	_____
23. Are prospects prequalified?	_____	_____	_____	_____
24. Is the pricing philosophy logical and well understood?	_____	_____	_____	_____
25. Does the bank have a long-term prospect solicitation view as opposed to a "quick hit" philosophy?	_____	_____	_____	_____
26. Are bankers responsible for intangibles such as quality and customer satisfaction?	_____	_____	_____	_____
Category B average _____				
C. Training and Development				
1. Are time and resources made available for training in such skills as time management, negotiating, interviewing, and listening?	_____	_____	_____	_____
2. Are basic skills periodically updated?	_____	_____	_____	_____
3. Is training routinely given in new or evolving issues?	_____	_____	_____	_____
4. Is training reinforced on the job?	_____	_____	_____	_____
5. Is an appropriate professional reading program encouraged?	_____	_____	_____	_____

	Evaluation (1 to 5)	Priority for Change (Use check or X) High	Deferred	Indefinite
C. Training and Development				
6. Is continuing education encouraged?	____	____	____	____
7. Is there a minimum inventory of skills for commercial bankers?	____	____	____	____
8. Are mentorships encouraged?	____	____	____	____
Category C average ____				
D. Departmental Administration				
1. Have assistants and receptionists been briefed on standardized routines such as telephone etiquette?	____	____	____	____
2. Do the manager and bankers meet periodically with administrative support to discuss workloads and other issues?	____	____	____	____
3. Is there a procedure for handling customer complaints?	____	____	____	____
4. Do the bankers periodically review data storage with administrative support?	____	____	____	____
5. Are copies of credit file comments and correspondence circulated among the bankers?	____	____	____	____
6. Are work priority conflicts that involve assistants discussed and resolved by the bankers?	____	____	____	____
Category D average ____				
E. Management Practices				
1. Do bankers receive adequate coaching and counseling on an ongoing basis?	____	____	____	____

	Evaluation (1 to 5)	Priority for Change (Use check or X)		
		High	Deferred	Indefinite
E. Management Practices				
2. Are pending loans and new prospects discussed informally and adequately in advance of formal proposals?	_____	_____	_____	_____
3. Is feedback given and received in the spirit of improving overall performance?	_____	_____	_____	_____
4. Is the manager readily available?	_____	_____	_____	_____
5. Are minimum performance standards established?	_____	_____	_____	_____
6. Are annual individual objectives established for each banker and are they updated quarterly?	_____	_____	_____	_____
7. Are performance appraisals effective?	_____	_____	_____	_____
8. Is salary administration logical and understood?	_____	_____	_____	_____
9. Are promotion policies logical, understood, and reflective of the appropriate culture?	_____	_____	_____	_____
10. Are intangible goals such as customer satisfaction valued?	_____	_____	_____	_____

Category E average _____

1500 1997
500 4/99
1000 9/00